GOD CHALLENGES THE DICTATORS
DOOM OF THE NAZIS PREDICTED

The Destruction of the Third Reich Foretold by the Director of Swansea Bible College an Intercessor from Wales

REES HOWELLS AND **MATHEW BACKHOLER**

God Challenges the Dictators, Doom of the Nazis Predicted
The Destruction of the Third Reich Foretold by the Director of
Swansea Bible College an Intercessor from Wales

ISBN 978-1-907066-77-1 (paperback) 2021
ISBN 978-1-907066-76-4 (hardback) 2020

British Library Cataloguing In Publication Data
A Record of this Publication is available from the British Library

First Published in June 2021 by ByFaith Media

JESUS CHRIST IS LORD

CONTENTS OF PHOTOS

CONTENTS

FOREWORD

For the Lord will not cast off His people, nor will He forsake His inheritance. But judgment will return to righteousness, and all the upright in heart will follow it. Who will rise up for me against the evildoers? Who will stand up for me against the workers of iniquity?' (Psalm 94:14-16).

God Challenges the Dictators: Doom of the Nazis Predicted (1939) was the only book written and published by Rees Howells, it is rare and difficult to obtain. Over the years I have been contacted by a number of people seeking a copy, and now for the first time in eighty years it is available, in a reformatted edition, fully annotated with digitally enhanced photos.

God Challenges the Dictators was translated into a number of languages including French, Spanish and German and copies or excerpts were printed and distributed around war-torn Europe. Through contacts, portions of the German edition: *Gott Gegen Die Diktatoren: Der Untergang der Nationalisozialisten Vorhergesagt* von Rees Howells, which translates as 'God Against the Dictators: The Fall of the National Socialists' by Rees Howells, were sent to leading members of the Nazi party including Adolf Hitler, Joseph Goebbels, Hermann Göring, Joachim von Ribbentrop, Rudulf Hess and Heinrich Himmler on New Year's Day 1940! In addition, as the Nazi régime was in control of much of Europe, excerpts of the book were read out over the Freedom Broadcasting Station – the secret radio which the Gestapo were trying to find![1]

British Prime Minister Neville Chamberlain who served from May 1937 to May 1940 was also sent a copy, alongside members of the government, as was Prime Minister Winston Churchill who served from May 1940 to July 1945. A Specimen Chapter of 32-pages was sent to 20,000 Ministers across Britain to encourage prayer and stimulate faith and strength in the midst of what seemed overwhelming odds.[2]

In the late 1990s, my brother and I joined the community of faith at the Bible College of Wales (BCW) which Rees Howells founded in Swansea, Wales in 1924. During our time as students and then staff, we became close to the elderly staff who knew and prayed with Rees Howells, many of whom had been part of the one hundred and twenty who had forsaken all nearly three years before the outbreak of World War II (1939-1945). They had laid down their lives and callings to be intercessors for the nations to help train students for Christian ministry. They lived through a time when Britain was surrounded by the Nazis and their Third Reich who were better equipped, militarily prepared and successful in their military campaigns.

The threat of war with Germany had been looming since 1936 in Britain and gasmasks were produced in the millions, beginning in 1938 and by September 1939, 38 million gasmasks had been issued to civilians across Britain. As early as December 1938, trenches were being dug in Hyde Park, London, England, and bomb shelters were being built due to the fear of attack and an inevitable war.

It may be hard to imagine in the present-day, but Britain was literally on the verge of being invaded and occupied within the lifetime of Rees Howells, his son Samuel Rees Howells and the other prayer warriors at the Bible College of Wales. It was within the context of a war brewing from the mid-1930s onwards and the possibility of invasion in 1938, 1939, 1940 (and spring 1942), that Rees Howells publicly declared in the newspapers that God was going to intervene, and as the situation grew worse into war, he wrote his conviction after war was declared in September 1939, in *God Challenges the Dictators.* This was published in December 1939 and mentioned in the newspapers in the unoccupied parts of Europe, America and as far away as Australia and some of the Oceanic Islands.

In a letter dated, 2nd November 1939, to A. J. Russell of London, Rees Howells' editor, he wrote: 'Now I have the manuscript [*God Challenges the Dictators*] nearly ready.... In my prediction I said there was going to be no European War, and the prediction was fulfilled when Italy, [and] Spain dropped out of it, and isolated Germany. This fulfilled my prediction....'[3]

Rees Howells lived for the fulfilment of Jesus' Great Commission (the Gospel to Every Creature) and he believed that Hitler and Mussolini, the dictators of Germany and Italy, would have to be defeated in order for the peaceful work of world evangelisation to continue. He also saw Stalin of Russia as a threat that God could use to defeat the other dictators, whilst all three dictators were allies! Hitler and Mussolini were part of the Axis powers of Berlin-Rome. Rees may not have anticipated how far things would have to go in a time of war for this to be fulfilled.

On 31st August 1939, the evacuation of children in towns and cities at risk from Nazi bombardment began and around three million children were evacuated in Britain! The following day saw the first night of the blackouts. Heavy black cloth had to cover all windows; light was not permitted to aid the enemy in aerial bombardments. Those with motor vehicles could only have a small portion of their headlights available to shine light onto the road ahead of them, which hindered visibility when all street lights and shop-front displays were turned off for six years.

The Conscription Bill was passed on 3rd September 1939, the day Britain declared war with Germany for invading Poland and ignoring Britain's ultimatum to withdraw from its Ally. In January 1940, the Government called for another million soldiers, all those from the ages of 19-28 to be conscripted which was rising close to three million.

A National Day of Prayer for the country was set aside for 8th September 1940 and church bells of the South and South West Counties of England rang in the morning as a warning of an attempted invasion! However, it proved to be a false alarm, but Britain was on edge and high alert, and Hitler and his storm-troopers wanted Christian England to submit to his will. Rees Howells and many other said, "No! God will save Christian England" and "bring the Nazis to their doom. God will not surrender Protestant Germany, the land of the Reformation, to Hitlerism (the Antichrist)."[4]

> 'I know your dwelling place, your going out and your coming in, and your rage against Me. Because your rage against Me and your tumult have come up to My ears, therefore I will put My hook in your nose and My bridle in your lips, and I will turn you back by the way which you came' (Isaiah 37:28-29).

Prime Minister Winston Churchill in his 'We Shall Fight on the Beaches' speech on 4th June 1940, declared, "...Even though large tracts of Europe and many old and famous States have fallen or may fall into the grip of the Gestapo and all the odious apparatus of Nazi rule, we shall not flag or fail. We shall go on to the end. We shall fight in France, we shall fight on the seas and oceans, we shall fight with growing confidence and growing strength in the air, we shall defend our Island, whatever the cost may be. We shall fight on the beaches, we shall fight on the landing grounds, we shall fight in the fields and in the streets, we shall fight in the hills; we shall never surrender...."

Prime Minister Winston Churchill in his 'Finest Hour Speech' on 18th June 1940, said, "...I expect that the Battle of Britain is about to begin. Upon this battle depends *the survival of Christian civilisation.* Upon it depends our own British life, and the long continuity of our institutions and our Empire. The whole fury and might of the enemy must very soon be turned on us. Hitler knows that he will have to break us in this Island or lose the war. If we can stand up to him, all Europe may be free and the life of the world may move forward into broad, sunlit uplands. But if we fail, then the whole world, including the United States, including all that we have known and cared for, will sink into the abyss of a new Dark Age made more sinister, and perhaps more protracted, by the lights of perverted science. Let us therefore brace ourselves to our duties, and so bear ourselves that, if the British Empire and its Commonwealth last for a thousand years, men will still say, 'This was their finest hour.' "

Six months after V.E. Day (Victory in Europe) Rees Howells wrote a letter dated, 7th November 1945, to Rev. S. H. Dixon of the Conference of Missionary Societies, in London: 'Dear Mr Dixon, thank you very much for your letter...I am enclosing you a copy of my book.... It was revealed to us that the Devil had entered into Hitler and those followers of his who are awaiting their trial today [Nuremberg Trials of 1st November 1945 to 1st October 1946], and that this war was not a European War, but that God challenged the Dictators. Keep this in your mind when you are reading it. The book is in two parts, and the predictions have become true....'[5]

'When you go to war in your land against the enemy who oppresses you, then you shall sound an alarm with the trumpets, and you will be remembered before the Lord your God, and you will be saved from your enemies' (Numbers 10:9).

PREFACE

'Defend the poor and fatherless; do justice to the afflicted and needy. Deliver the poor and needy; free them from the hand of the wicked' (Psalm 82:3-4).

In Rees Howells' book *God Challenges the Dictators* (1939) he predicted the doom of the dictators, at a time when they seemed unstoppable. They were winning battles in a matter of weeks, and taking territory, which Germany had failed to achieve in years during the First World War (1914-1918). But Rees was persistent – they would be defeated.

As we look back, we can also testify to a remarkable series of events, which led to his book being translated into German and 'prophetically seeded' into the offices of Hitler and senior Nazi leaders. Extracts from Rees Howells' book were additionally read out on the Freedom Broadcasting Station via radio to the German people. Such prophetic symbolism is reminiscent of the Old Testament prophets (Jeremiah 43:9-13 and Ezekiel 4:1-17).

Apart from Rees Howells' war predictions, he also declared that the work of world evangelisation would continue again until fulfilment, that Germany would return to be a great missionary-sending nation and that the evangelical witness would survive in Germany. He foresaw 10,000 people who would open themselves fully to the Holy Spirit to be channels of God's blessing to the world, and that money would be released like manna, for the completion of the Great Commission – to reach Every Creature with the Gospel in his generation (Mark 16:15).

Rees Howells foresaw the growing threat from Stalin and the Soviet Union, proposing that he may "be the greatest foe to the Church the world has ever known." The history of the Cold War (1947-1991) and the fierce persecution of Christians by the Communists bear testimony to his words.[1]

Rees Howells backed up his predictions with testimonies from the past. He had prophesied and then accomplished the building of the largest Bible College in Britain, by faith alone. He achieved this without making appeals for partners, or urging people to give without pausing to think. On occasions he would politely turn down financial offers of help, or even return money, if he felt it should not have been given to him. He wanted to prove that faith and prayer were sufficient to build a work for the Lord, without any claim of manipulation.

The numerous gifts he received, including the famous gift of £10,000 in July 1938 (worth £674,400 in 2020) were evidence to Rees Howells that he heard from God and was obedient to the Holy Spirit. These gifts arrived within the context of several economic catastrophes Britain was living through – the colossal outlay of the nation from the First World War (1914-1918), the lingering costs of the Great Depression and the foreshadowing of invasion by the Nazi régime.

After the 'General European War' widened, something which Rees believed would be avoided, he continued to promote his book which was published in mid-December 1939. He believed that *God Challenges the Dictators* should be read in the light of the greater revelations within the arc of the book, rather than the specifics written in a moment of history. This is why he continued to encourage the spread of the book, as a work of profound testimony, even after the war ended in Europe in May 1945.

Rees Howells saw no contradiction in his initial belief that the war would be shortened, then prolonged, if it was for a greater purpose. God had promised the defeat of the dictators when it seemed impossible and He would complete the work. Critics may point to Rees' developing interpretation of 'No European War' of 1936 and 1938 to 'No General European War' of 1939, and the struggle to interpret this into the 1940s, with the changing alliances in the global politics of the time, which led to a World War, however it was Nazi Germany versus every country in Europe, apart from those nations that remained neutral. In March 1936, Hitler broke the Locarno Treaty and marched his Nazi troops into the 'demilitarised' Rhineland, a buffer zone, and war could have broken out then when most European countries were militarily unprepared. From April 1936, the 'crisis of war in Europe,' wrote Norman Grubb, was averted and 'changed into a search for peace; when the proposal was made for a twenty-five year Peace Pact.' Whilst peace talks gave Britain time to breath, Rees Howells was not fooled, as Hitler was hell-bent on conquering Christian Europe.

'It was in March 1936,' wrote Norman Grubb 'that Mr [Rees] Howells began to see clearly that Hitler was Satan's agent for preventing the Gospel going to Every Creature.' Rees Howells later said, "In fighting Hitler we have always said that we were not up against man, but the Devil. Mussolini is man, but Hitler is different. He can tell the day this 'spirit' came into him." Rees knew that to see the Gospel to Every Creature Vision fulfilled, Hitler and the other dictators must be destroyed.[2]

In September 1938, the Munich Pact was signed between Britain's Mr Neville Chamberlain and Germany's Adolf Hitler concerning Czechoslovakia being overrun by the Nazis. Hitler had also wanted to invade Britain in October 1938, egged on by his generals and senior officials. Hitler himself went against the voice of Satan, his inner guide, as God bent him to His sovereign will. The British Ambassador to Germany, Sir Neville Henderson would later recall how Hitler somewhat bitterly said to Chamberlain, "You are the only man to whom I have ever made a concession."[3]

However, if war had broken out in 1936, 1937 or 1938, Britain was unprepared, something that Winston Churchill had said for many years as Nazi Germany built up its military force and arsenal. To sum up the theme of the Volume 1 of *The Second World War: The Gathering Storm* (1948), Winston Churchill wrote: 'How the English speaking-peoples through their unwisdom, carelessness and good nature allowed the wicked to rearm.'

For Rees Howells, the dictators would fall and if his reputation was diminished, that too was a good thing. As John the Baptist declared, "Jesus must increase, but I must decrease" (John 3:30). Whilst Jesus said, "Unless a grain of wheat falls into the ground and dies, it remains alone; but if it dies, it produces much grain" (John 12:24). Rees' desire to reach Every Creature within a thirty year period, laid claims that he overreached the promises made to him, however it was a good focus to drive towards, as 'the fields are white unto harvest' (John 4:35) and 'how shall they hear without a preacher?' (Romans 10:14).

My brother and I were privileged to live for some years in the community that Rees Howells founded, the Bible College in Swansea. We became friends with those who knew and prayed alongside Rees and sat under the ministry of his son, Samuel Rees Howells for many years. When we read the book *God Challenges the Dictators*, my brother and I ask, "What can we learn from Rees Howells' experience?" Those who shout, "Heresy," at others used by God, are rarely in the right spirit to hear from, or know the guidance of the Spirit.[4]

Jesus turned and rebuked him saying, "You do not know what manner of spirit you are of" (Luke 9:55). Jesus warned, "Judge not, that you be not judged. For with what judgment you judge, you will be judged; and with the measure you use, it will be measured back to you" (Matthew 7:1-2). It's important to appreciate that the disciples of Jesus believed for several years that He was presently building an earthly 'Kingdom of Israel' and they called upon the Old Testament prophets to justify their belief (Acts 1:6).

Rees Howells was a prophetic pioneer. He had no wise elder in the Church to consult – with experience in healing, prophecy or in the life of faith. As a pioneer in the gifts of the Spirit, we should in humility expect that he, like us, had lessons to learn, and it is always possible to overstep a revelation or to go beyond one's faith. How many accused Malachi of exaggeration when he prophesied, "The Lord, whom you seek, will suddenly come to His temple?" (Malachi 3:1). Four hundred years later, the Lord Jesus came, at a time when few were expecting Him! In New Testament times, many early believers preached the imminent return of Christ and were confused with the delay (2 Peter 3:4). These were not heretics; they lived with their feet on the ground and their eyes on the edge of eternity.

One of the greatest lessons to be drawn from Rees Howells' text is to never limit God to a certain timescale and possible scenarios. Several times Rees gave specific dates to the fulfilments of God's plan when speaking in public, and sometimes in the text he attempts to guess how Hitler and the Nazi regime will fall. The Apostle Paul conveys that we know in part and see in part (1 Corinthians 13:9, 12). Consequently, we must not add to, nor take away, from the revelation of the Lord.

Critics of the prophetic Church may embrace the spirit of judgment and quote the Old Testament punishments, for predictions that result in an unexpected manifestation. They forget that in the Church age no such severity is demanded; instead we are urged to test and try all things (1 Thessalonians 5:21). The Prophet Jonah denounced the cruel Assyrians in the city of Nineveh and declared the word of the Lord, "Yet forty days and Nineveh shall be overthrown!" The king took this seriously and the people humbled themselves and wore sackcloth and sat in ashes as a sign of humility, and a revival ensued, as God relented from the disaster He said would befall them! (Jonah 3). I wonder if there were some who denounced Jonah as a false prophet, because the Ninevites repented and turned from their wicked ways? Was it not ironic that Jonah himself set about to see the destruction of the cruel Assyrians who did not know their right from their left, whilst God cared about this great city? (Jonah 4).

The prophets of the early Church weighed their words and kept each other accountable to the revelation given to all (Acts 13:1 and 1 Corinthians 14:29-31). None were persecuted or defamed in this process. When Agabus prophesied a famine in Judea, the church responded immediately to take up an offering to help (Acts 11:27-30), but the timing was off. They responded too soon and the gift was received before there was any semblance of need. But the famine did come.

If Rees Howells had been able to confer with other prophetic people, they may have urged him to remain within the wider revelation of 'God Challenges the Dictators: Doom of the Nazis Predicted.' This was an outrageous prophecy in itself, when we evaluate military reality. Adding the specifics of when, or how, undermined the arc of the revelation. However, Rees gloried in the 'death of one's reputation,' believing there is more to be learned in perceived public failure, than in success. "Woe to you when all men speak well of you," said the Lord (Luke 6:26).

Rees Howells also limited himself to a thirty year period to reach the world with the Gospel. Whilst this was common practice for ministries to declare what could be achieved in the following decades, or a generation, with hindsight, it became polemical. Spiritual pessimism found no place in Rees' view of what was possible through fully surrendered vessels to be used for God's glory.

What is clear is that Rees Howells and his intercessors were pleading for the Gospel to go to Every Creature and the changes in the world testify to the power of their intercessions. Quoting from the sequel to *Rees Howells Intercessor* (1952) by Norman Grubb, we learn the following from *Samuel Rees Howells: A Life of Intercession* (2012) by Richard Maton: 'In 1900, there were 7.5 million Christians in Africa, today there are 505 million. In South America in 1900, there were only 700,000 Bible believing Christians, today there are 93 million. In Asia in 1900, believers numbered 22 million, today they consist of almost 400 million!'

Rees Howells believed that after Germany was freed from the Nazis, its young people would be used mightily in the Every Creature harvest. During this period of intercession in Rees' life, a child was born in Germany in 1940 named Reinhard Bonnke and by 1959, he was planted as a 'prophetic seed,' at the Bible College of Wales (BCW). As a student under Samuel Rees Howells, Reinhard was walking in the College grounds pondering his future. In a despondent state he told the Lord, "Oh Lord, I'm not a teacher, I'm not a preacher, I'm not a pastor, I'm not an evangelist." The moment Reinhard said, "I'm not an evangelist," the Holy Spirit spoke to him and said, "But I have called you to be an evangelist." From that moment on, he knew his calling and after his three years of training he left Rees Howells' campus to go on to lead tens of millions to Christ through CFaN.

'The glory of Swansea Bible College was that it forced us to live by faith,' wrote Reinhard Bonnke. 'We prayed for everything. For the huge supply of winter coal necessary to heat our buildings, to the bus fare to take us street preaching at the weekend. The school [of faith / College] supplied only food and lodging for us. We were instructed to 'pray in' all the extras. And always, we were required to pray in secret without publicly mentioning our needs. This had been George Müller's legacy and the legacy of Rees Howells as well. Now Rees' son Samuel followed the faith path. I learned to embrace it. Whenever a student or staff member saw their need met by the Lord they would testify about it. These stories were meant to encourage the other students to live in complete dependence upon God. The phrase that was used when God met a need was "I've been delivered." '[5]

Students from Rees Howells' Bible College reached the ends of the earth with the Gospel and the ongoing fruit of his ministry continues today. Consequently, when we read *God Challenges the Dictators*, we must understand that Rees was a mighty man of faith, and there are things we can learn from his highs and lows.

Rees Howells was correct in predicting that, "God is going to destroy Hitler and the Nazi regime," and his ministry did prove, "Prayer and faith," to be "efficient agents" to build a ministry. Rees found how to "change God's promises into current coin," and built an organisation free from exploitative emotional appeals. Rees may have overstepped the revelation when he thought a war could be avoided or shortened, but he was not ashamed of delay. When the war expanded to a general and then World War, people questioned Rees. To the cynic – unaware of the ways of the Spirit in the process of death to self – there was no other conclusion than Rees had failed and cannot be trusted. For Rees, he saw the power of death and resurrection at work once again. He said, "The glory and the credit for victory in this war must come to the Holy Spirit and not to man. God has declared war on the Devil and it is God who will give the victory."[6]

In response to criticism, Rees Howells took the College staff through the story of Moses, who had declared to the Hebrews slaves that their deliverance was at hand. What followed was the humiliation of Moses by the Hebrews – the persecution worsened and they criticised Moses for telling them that "God" has spoken to him (Exodus 5:20-23 and Deuteronomy 5:20). Similar themes reoccurred throughout the escape from Egypt when they were initially halted at the Red Sea (Exodus 14:11-14), and the wilderness journey when the people were 'almost ready to stone Moses' over lack of water (Exodus 17:1-4), and complained and wept as they 'yielded to intense cravings' for Egyptian food (Exodus 11:1-10, 18-20).

When things become harder than expected in the Lord's work, God's people have a tendency to forget past miracles and descend into bitter criticism of God's servants. Moses and Jesus were deemed as unreliable prophets (Exodus 17:2-4) and they wanted to throw Jesus off a cliff (Luke 4:24-29) and on another occasion stone Him (John 8:57-59).

In moments of struggle, Rees took courage from Judges 20, where the predictions of victory, were followed by two defeats, prolonged battles and failure. Nevertheless, the Lord's servants were vindicated, despite long delays, unexpected setbacks and defeats. Even the Lord's ministry was a disappointment to those hoping for more: 'But we were hoping that it was He who was going to redeem Israel' (Luke 24:20-21).

During this struggle, Rees Howells pronounced in May 1940, "If I had a choice again about making this prediction [when the war would end], I would make it tonight, although it has gone much farther than we thought it would.... We shall never defend the prediction. The point is – can God put a doubt in us who have really believed? If the Lord tells you that this delay is for His glory, then you must take victory in it. There is no glory in delay, unless there was faith to put it through. I can really thank Him for the delay. I wouldn't be without this experience for the world. Very strange, that what is death in the eyes of the world, is victory to the Holy Spirit. We could never have had a greater death than in this prediction being delayed. But we are not going to have resurrection on one point more than has gone to the cross."[7]

When Samuel Rees Howells asked Normal Grubb to write a book about the life of his dad, Rees Howells, many friends of Grubb encouraged him to avoid the story of a man, who had 'discredited' himself in their eyes and said his name (Grubb's) and ministry should not be associated with that man. The names of those critics are forgotten, but the story of Rees Howells and the lessons he learnt – through his successes and failures – have touched the lives of millions of people.

We invite you to ponder *God Challenges the Dictators* in a spirit of humility and wisdom. Not to allow the spirit of judgment to possess you, but to discern what we all can learn from Rees Howells' life and to especially read the annotations in the back of the book under Sources and Notes. He walked a life of faith in the Spirit that few others have and the peak of his ministry of intercession was reached after this book was published. The war had already commenced before Rees Howells began to write *God Challenges the Dictators* and he was adamant that it should be published and read, in the light of its greater revelation.

The Bible is filled with people God used who were fallible. The 'saints' of the Bible lived extraordinary lives of faith, despite the shadow of their faults. The Lord did not cast aside Peter when he made a mistake and denied the Lord, nor did He despise His disciples who ran away from Him in the worst moment of His life, or doubting Thomas who missed Jesus after the resurrection and would not believe unless he saw and put his hands into Jesus' wounds. In John 8:7, we are told that 'casting the first stone,' is permitted only for those who are without fault, but to realise that 'all have sinned and fall short of the glory of God' (Romans 3:23).

Rees Howells walked higher mountains of faith than most ever will and there is much to learn in the entirety of Rees Howells' experiences. Think and ponder. Listen and pray. Be wise in the Lord and honour those whom the Lord has used in mighty exploits.

The brothers, Paul and Mathew Backholer.

ByFaith Media (www.ByFaith.org).

The monetary figures for the year 2020 have been included within the text in parenthesis [ ] to give a contemporary value of costs and are calculated using the Bank of England's inflation calculator. They are based on the year an amount is mentioned; therefore £100 in 1924 with inflation calculated for 2020 would be different than £100 in 1932 or for 1939. When this paperback was first published in 2021, the Bank of England's Bank Rate was at an all-time low of 0.1% (January 2021), meaning any financial changes over a single year from 2020 are negligible.[8]

A 1939 dustcover / jacket from Rees Howells' book converted into greyscale. The original colour is black with white lettering, with the continents in white, whilst the oceans and rays are in red. The cost was 1 shilling (1/-). Round 2 shilling stickers (2/-) were placed over the circle denoting the price difference between the card cover edition and the hardback edition. This was the most economical way rather than having two sets of artwork. Some editions of the hardback do not have the 2 shilling stickers on its dustcover. Incidentally, when Rees Howells went to buy Glynderwen Estate in 1923 he *only* had 2 shillings in his pocket.

INTRODUCTION

This is an unusual book. It differs in many respects from any book that has been written in this generation. Because it contains a number of prophecies which concern everybody, some of which have already come true, we believe that it is essentially a book for all to read and ponder deeply. It may bring much good to many people. If it does no more than give vision and a sure foothold to some who are wrapped in mists and walking uncertainly, it will have served a useful purpose at this time of crisis.

We are assured that it will do much more, for it has a vital message for many nations. It has an especial message for you in this country, and if you believe it, you may be comforted "by the comfort wherewith we ourselves are comforted of God" (2 Corinthians 1:4). We have not been afraid nor dismayed since it was revealed to us, "for the battle is the Lord's.... Stand ye still and see the deliverance of the Lord with you" (2 Chronicles 20:15, 17).

In the second part of the book, the predictions described concern the founding and development of a Bible College, Bible College Schools, Hospital, etc. These are given in order to show the reader the many years it has taken the College to come to know the voice of God, and to give those greater and wider predictions that relate to war and peace, the rise and fall of dictators, and epochal events that are yet to be. It does not shy at those immensities which are of absorbing interest to all. Moreover what is written here is not mere guesswork, but the sure word of prophecy, proof that God still speaks through His servants, and shows them things that are to come.

The title, *God Challenges the Dictators,* and its subtitle, *Doom of Nazis Predicted*, convey at once to the reader the reason why the book is sent out at this time. Keep it by you and check future events with what is here recorded.[1]

On that fatal day, September 1st 1939, Hitler hurled this defiance at the world:

"As a National Socialist and a German soldier I enter upon this struggle (war with Poland) with a stout heart.... One word I have never learned: that is, surrender. I have once more put on that coat that was the most sacred and dear to me. I will not take it off again until victory is secured or I will not survive the outcome."[2]

Our Prime Minister in his well-balanced and temperate broadcast to the German People on September 4th, said,
"I regret to have to say it – that nobody in this country any longer places any trust in your leader's word. He gave his word that he would respect the Locarno Treaty; he broke it. [In March 1936, Adolf Hitler sent his soldiers into the Rhineland, a demilitarised zone and broke the Locarno Treaty which had been signed at the end of World War I (1914-1918)]. He gave his word that he neither wished nor intended to annex Austria; he broke it [12 March 1938]. He declared that he would not incorporate the Czechs in the Reich; he did so [29 September 1938 and invaded on 15 March 1939]. He gave his word after Munich [30 September 1938] that he had no further territorial demands in Europe; he broke it. He gave his word that he wanted no Polish provinces; he broke it [he annexed a number of provinces in October 1938, making what became known as the Danzig Corridor or the Polish Corridor]. He has sworn to you for years [views made public since the mid-1920s] that he was the mortal enemy of Bolshevism; he is now its ally [23 August 1939, with the Hitler-Stalin Pact]. Can you wonder his word is, for us, not worth the paper it is written on?
"In this war we are not fighting against you, the German people, for whom we have no bitter feeling, but against a tyrannous and forsworn régime which has betrayed not only its own people but the whole of Western civilisation and all that you and we hold dear. *May God defend the right.*"

Mr Chamberlain had previously said, "There is hardly anything that I would not sacrifice for Peace, but one thing I must except, that is the liberty that we have enjoyed for hundreds of years, and which we will not surrender," and the whole of the British Empire stood behind him by saying, "Hitler's Peace we unitedly reject."
God also predicted beforehand through the College, that He will not surrender Protestant Germany, the land of the Reformation, to Hitlerism (the Antichrist). So, if Hitler says that he will die before he will surrender, the Allies that they will not surrender, and God says that He will not surrender, this war is going to be a fight to a finish – "the survival of the fittest."

This introduction was written during the very weekend when the German magnetic mines were beginning to blow up British and neutral ships. Only a week before, Mr Churchill had said over the wireless that we had cleared the high-seas, and not a German ship was to be seen, that our blockade [which began in September 1939] was nearly perfect and complete; and then suddenly came the magnetic mines [November 1939]. Shocked at this unexpected blow we consoled ourselves by saying we had struck a bad patch. Yet Hitler has boasted that Germany has other diabolical inventions to unloose. But don't be alarmed at Nazi threats.

"Man's extremity is God's opportunity." When God told the College on September 9th, 1939 to send a prediction to the *Daily Press* that "God will Intervene in a Miraculous Way to End the War" – had God then foreseen that man could not end it? Is the day coming when our country will have to look to God, and to Him alone, to deliver us from this black spectre of Hitlerism? Will God have to step in as He did in Biblical times to deliver our nation, because we are fighting solely for freedom and religious liberty? Although we show clearly in the early chapters of this book that God has promised to "intervene to end the war," we have many a setback before He does so.

Open your Bibles to the Book of Judges to where God told Israel to go against Benjamin, because they refused to give up those men who had committed a certain folly in their tribe (Judges 19-20). And it is for exactly the same reason that England and France have gone against Germany, asking them to give up those Nazi leaders who have committed crime after crime against their own people, the German Jews, and the smaller nations round them, the Czechs, the Poles, and the Austrians.

The Benjamites in all only numbered twenty-six thousand men that drew sword, while Israel (Judah) numbered four hundred thousand men that drew sword. God was with Israel, and sent them against Benjamin, but Benjamin killed the first day no less than twenty-two thousand men. The second day again the Benjamites killed of the Israelites eighteen thousand men that drew sword; so in two days these sturdy fighters had killed forty thousand – nearly double their own number! But remember this – the Benjamites were fighting for their lives, while Israel (Judah) was only fighting for a principle. This seems to be a true illustration of the war today between Germany and the Allies. Whilst we are fighting for a principle, Hitler and the Nazis are fighting for their lives; the Nazis do desperate things because they are a thousand times more desperate than we are. Hitler knows well that he is making a last bid to save his life of crime, as do his Nazi leaders whose consciences must give them much uneasiness; and they will use every evil device to help them, as they did in Poland, and are now doing with their magnetic mines in the North Sea.

So Christian England will have to do today as the Israelites did in their day: "The children of Israel inquired of the Lord, saying, 'Shall I yet again go out to battle against the children of Benjamin my brother, or shall I cease?' And the Lord said, "Go up; for tomorrow I will deliver them into thine hand" (Judges 20:28). It may be that we, like the Israelites, will have to cry out to God in our extremity for the help, which will certainly come. The Benjamites made their last desperate bid to save the tribe, but God wiped them out on that day. And it may be the same with Germany, who are today intact (for so far it has only been a war of blockade), and they will have to be desperate indeed before they will voice the word "surrender." For have not all the Nazi leaders, like Hitler, pledged themselves to die before they surrender? They know already what is coming to them.

This Book of Predictions is nothing if not opportune. May it be a warning to England to stand to the end under the shadow of the Almighty, and to obey His constant guidance. May we cry to God as did the people of Nineveh when Jonah predicted their doom. The ruler of that mighty city "arose from his throne, and he laid his robe from him, and covered him with sackcloth, and sat in ashes," and he called all his people to "cry mightily unto God: yea, let them turn everyone from his evil way.... And God saw their works, that they turned from their evil way; and God repented of the evil....and He did it not" (Jonah 3:1-10).

If God saved wicked Nineveh when it repented and cried for help, He will save Christian England, and He will even save the Modernists in Germany (the New Theologians), who have made such a mockery of the Book of Jonah. Even though their New Theology, so misled them, today these "Reverend Storm Troopers" would be ready to sit in the seat of the Ninevites, in "sackcloth and ashes," repenting of their folly in handling the Word of the Lord so lightly.

If they had followed their own countryman "Saint George Müller" (1805-1898) they, like him, would really believed that the Bible was the Word of God. That modern "St. George" [patron Saint of England] made Orphanages in Christian England, maintaining two thousand orphaned children by prayer and faith alone, to be a great object lesson to all. He drew out of God's Treasury a million and-a-half pounds without a single appeal to man. And the Bible College of Wales which issues this book, and which works on the same principles, will also draw out of God's Treasury Millions of pounds to carry out its own Vision: "The Gospel to Every Creature in the next twenty-five Years."[3]

If every man and woman in Christian England will cry to God as the Ninevites did, and continue to cry until God will answer, God will intervene as He did in Bible times, and raise England again to be His chosen power for evangelising the world.

The sending out of this Book of Predictions, in the darkest hour of the war, has cost more to the Founders of the College [Rees and Lizzie Howells] that any of the former predictions. Predictions are always open to criticism until their fulfilment. Many of the Prophets of old were put in prison, like Jeremiah and Micaiah, until their predictions were fulfilled. Then those who disbelieved and criticised were condemned, and the Prophets were praised. So the College will be fully compensated for any criticism, if the hundreds of thousands of wives, mothers and children who will be separated from their loved ones this Christmas, will take comfort in knowing that God is on their side; that He will bring their loved ones back again, when peace will be upon the earth, and goodwill towards men.[4]

> Fierce may be the conflict
> Strong may be the foe,
> But the King's own army
> None can overthrow.
> Round His standard ranging,
> Victory is secure,
> For His truth unchanging
> Makes the triumph sure.[5]

CHAPTER 1

God Versus the Dictators

Since March 1936, the Western democracies have done everything in their power to avoid a clash with the dictators. Meanwhile, the dictators under a cloak of National Revival in their countries, have been scheming and planning among themselves to dominate the world by force and bloodshed.

Before the 1914 War there was only one autocratic Government in Europe, and that was Russia. For centuries there had been a struggle between Monarchism and Republicanism; whether kings by heredity or the masses were to rule.

People who had emigrated to America from monarchical countries, like Russia and Germany, found liberty, because the people of the U.S.A. were ruling the destiny of that great country through their representatives in Congress and their Presidents whom they elected every four years.

George Washington, who won liberty and independence for America, said: "The nation which is incapable of winning its Parliamentary freedom is unworthy to exist." The common people should, through their deputies, be ruling the national destiny. That was why Lincoln brought in the Act of Emancipation, so that not even the rich should rule over any man, whether he be black-skinned or white. "The wind shall blow and the rain shall fall," said he, "on no man who goes forth to unrequited toil."

Those who emigrated from Russia to the United States found a wonderful freedom, and men like Lenin and others went back to their country and preached revolution and Communism. They were willing to risk their lives to emancipate two hundred million peasants out of the bondage of an autocratic Czar.[1]

In the uprising that followed hundreds of thousands were killed, others were exiled to Siberia, or deported; yet no military force could ever extinguish the urge for liberty now greatly stirring in the Russian people.

WESLEY SAVES ENGLAND

It was through Wesley's Revival [the Evangelical Revival 1739-1791][2] that England in the eighteenth century was saved from a revolution and a civil war. Ferocious laws figured on the Statute

Book; justice itself was cruel and vindictive. Judges swore on the Bench, and even chaplains cursed while they preached. Men who refused to plead on capital charge were pressed to death; and up to the year 1794, when the vicious law was repealed, women were publicly flogged.

At this dark period of our history the Church of England had lost its power. The clergy were discredited and our public life was flagrantly corrupt. In those dark days, only a spiritual revolution could save England. It came through God raising up John Wesley (1703-1791)[3] for his colossal task. Only another Wesley can save Germany, Russia or Italy, the countries of the military dictators, today.

THE UNHOLY ALLIANCE

In twenty years two menacing figures, Hitler and Stalin, have given their countries a greater set-back than England has progressed by the last two centuries of civilisation. Before Wesley's Revival, our Parliament was unreformed; two-thirds of the House of Commons were elected by the privileged rich, like the Duke of Norfolk, who nominated eleven members, Lord Lonsdale, nine members; and so on.

No less than three hundred M.P.s were returned by one hundred and sixty persons, while large cities were unrepresented by even a single member. Whilst politics were at a low ebb, Christianity was a living force, and the conscience of the masses was deeply quickened. Christianity was re-born in the individual heart, and the country, awakened to the truth of the Gospel, found again that it was the "power of God unto Salvation to all who believe" (Romans 1:16). Once again it was more than an outworn creed and a dead ritual; it was the thing most needful in life.

Hardly a branch of the social life of our country was unaffected by that Revival. The new effort to establish the Reign of God on earth reached to the Universities, the Army, the Navy and to every class of people. Even politics responded to the Revival. The Secret Ballot came, and at last the masses controlled the destiny of England. King Edward VII (1841-1910) and his Prime Minister, Sir Henry Campbell-Bannerman (1836-1908) were both democrats, in no way inferior to any President and Premier of the French Republic. King George V (1865-1936) was also a great democrat and so also is our present King. But countries like Russia and Germany, who were ruled by sword and rifle, by Czar and Kaiser (titles which meant the same – Cæsar) were, through their Socialist leaders, reduced to a state of revolution and civil war, to gain the liberty they saw here, in America and other democratic countries. Great changes came to them and to Italy as well. But in these changes, which are only transition stages, they have fallen into the hands of ambitious dictators, who have ruled the masses by a vile discipline, by rod and revolver, and secret police, destroying both Parliament and Democracy, and replacing these by a reign of terror, more or less terrible according to country, under their respective dictators.

STALIN

These three dictators have undergone amazing experiences. They have suffered much themselves, but have exacted from their fellows a hundredfold more. Stalin, the man from Georgia [formerly part of the Russian Empire], escaped from prison six times. Once he was in exile near the Arctic Sea, in Kuleika, which he called the empire of eternal snow. It was while there, he says, that even his stubborn nature was broken. His life among "dangerous criminals," and the silence of the north, transformed that fiery rebel into a very quiet man. But it did not change his evil nature.

When, after Lenin's death, Stalin came to power, he soon deported his rival, Trotsky, the man who, through his writings, had brought Soviet Russia into being. Trotsky too, had suffered much, he had been twice deported, had spent four years in a dungeon, and altogether had passed over twelve years in prison under the late Czar. Under Lenin he built up the Red Army, and sincerely endeavoured to give Russia the widest democracy. Because Trotsky maintained that Stalin's methods were only an imitation of the autocratic rule of the Czars – "ruling from above the masses below," Stalin plotted against Trotsky. When illness came, and Trotsky could not defend himself, Stalin exiled him, and deprived him of Soviet citizenship. Trotsky then had to live in the only country that would offer him refuge, Mexico.

During Stalin's bloody purge, every one of his fellow Revolutionists who took a leading part in Lenin's Government, were executed, and likewise everyone who had dared oppose the ambitions of this peasant dictator from Georgia. When a youth, Stalin had passed four years in an Orthodox Seminary at Tiflis, but the only use he made of the Christianity he was there taught was to put down the Church of God, and to replace God's Sabbath by a weekly pagan holiday.

This then is the man who has planned to impose his savagery on the Christian democracies. But as sure as there will come the downfall of Hitler and the Nazi régime – for God has revealed it – the time will also come when Stalin will pay the full price of his murderous life. God said to Cain: "The voice of thy brother's blood crieth unto Me from the ground and now thou art cursed" (Genesis 4:10).

The Devil has used and may yet use this man to be the greatest foe to the Church that the world has ever known, but the stone that Daniel saw, in his tremendous vision: "The stone that was cut out of the mountain without hands" (Daniel 2:45), will break in pieces this Stalin and the other blood-thirsty dictators as well.

MUSSOLINI

The fate of modern Italy was decided when Mussolini mobilised the Fascist forces, and threatened to march on Rome. The Italian Government resigned, whereupon the King of Italy invited Mussolini to form a Government; so the Duce became dictator of the new Italy. The old proportional representative system was done away with, and a new electoral law was put in force, parading the dictator's slogan: "Let parties die and the country be saved," and so the Fascist Totalitarian State was brought into being.

Mussolini proceeded to make war on Libya [in North Africa] and Abyssinia [now Ethiopia, in Africa]. When Germany decided to aid Italy in Abyssinia and Spain; Italy passed laws against the Jews. And so the Axis was formed. Italy then demanded Corsica [an island close to Italy and France], Nice [in Southern France] and Tunis [in North Africa]; and she took Albania [to the right of Italy, on the Balkan Peninsula in south-eastern Europe]. Italy had also helped Franco to overthrow the Liberal Government in Spain, and the Nazis rejoiced at the great danger thereby created for us in the Mediterranean. So, slowly but surely, the Berlin-Rome and Spanish Axis was forged, and only God, and God alone, could have foreseen that it had no sure foundation and would soon snap before our astonished eyes.

It was a tragedy that German support of Italy should have brought about the downfall of Abyssinia, a country known in Scripture as Ethiopia. Yet Ethiopia had been opened to the Gospel, and her missionaries were welcomed by the Emperor;

and it seemed that the Bible prophecy was coming true: "Princes shall come out of Egypt; *Ethiopia shall soon stretch out her hands unto God"* (Psalm 68:31). But for a time it seems the door there has been shut against the Gospel.

ITALY MAY CHANGE

However, from the day the Berlin-Rome Axis was broken, Italy began to turn to the democracies for refuge and help against Bolshevism and Soviet Russia, which are being used in the plan of God to break the evil Nazi régime, by stopping their further penetration into the Balkan and Baltic States.

ADOLF HITLER

Enough has been said in the Government's "Blue Paper" and "White Paper" concerning the "Treatment of German Nationals in Germany," to reveal the bestial and brutal treatment of human beings by Hitler and his co-assassins the "power-drunk adventurers of the Third Reich." Adolf Hitler, the German dictator in less than six months after coming to power, abolished the provincial governments, suppressed or murdered all political parties except the National Socialists, who are the only party in Germany today. Whoever attempts to organise another political party is punished with imprisonment or death.

Like Stalin, Hitler soon began to lift up his bloodstained hand against the Church of God. He has bitterly persecuted the Evangelical Churches. He regards allegiance to any other ruler than himself – even the God of Heaven – as treason. If the Evangelical Church sets God above the State, and worships Him and not the dictator, as it must do, its members are imprisoned like political offenders. Hitler the Antichrist appointed the Army Chaplain Müller[4] (1883-1945), who has bowed the knee to Baal, to be Reich Bishop [in 1933] to carry out his decrees, as did the Satraps in the time of Darius of old. It was these Satraps, who accused Daniel before the King of Babylon, saying that they actually "found Daniel praying and making supplication before his God," and not to the King, so they forced him to cast Daniel into the den of lions, though even the heathen King was sorry and said: "Thy God whom thou servest continually, He will deliver thee" (Daniel 6:16). And He did.

HITLER'S FATE

The Bible College has predicted that the God of Daniel will deliver Pastor Niemöller[5] (1892-1984) and the hundreds of other German Evangelicals who have followed him to the concentration camps (Hitler's dens of lions). It affirms that their places will one day be occupied by the fanatical Nazi leaders, "the power-drunk adventurers," if any of them escape a speedy death. Just as Darius treated those who accused Daniel, so will the Nazis be treated, for they have afflicted Germany and God's servants most sore.

After the downfall of the Nazi régime there will be a new Government in a new Protestant Germany. It will cause men to "tremble and fear" before the God of Martin Luther and the God of Martin Niemöller: "For He is the living God, and steadfast for ever, and His Kingdom that which shall not be destroyed, and His dominion shall be even unto the end" (Daniel 6:26). So then, the God who delivereth His people, will deliver the oppressed in Germany, the land of the Reformation, and will call out again from that enslaved country thousands of missionaries afire for God to take the Gospel to Every Creature.

THE HEAD OF GOLD

God passed judgment on the proud Kings of Babylon, and through Daniel he said of Nebuchadnezzar (the "Head of Gold" of the famous image): "Thou, O king, art a king of kings: for the God of Heaven hath given thee a kingdom, power and strength and glory. And wheresoever the children of men dwell...hath He given into thine hand, and hath made thee ruler over them all. *Thou art this head of gold*" (Daniel 2:37-38). But when that ancient Overlord challenged his three Hebrew governors – Shadrach, Meshach and Abednego, saying: "Do not ye serve my gods, nor worship the golden image which I have set up? Who is that God that shall deliver you out of my hands?" The answer they gave to their proud king is now going to ring out through Germany: "Our God whom we serve is able to deliver us from the burning fiery furnace, and He will deliver us out of thine hand, O Hitler."

When he saw "the form of the fourth like the Son of God" walking in the fiery furnace with the brave Hebrew servants of the Living God, who were thus triumphantly delivered, the King of Babylon made a solemn decree "that every people, nation and language, which speak anything amiss against the God of Shadrach, Meshach and Abednego, shall be cut in pieces, and their houses be made a dunghill, because there is no other God that can deliver after this sort" (Daniel 3:29).

THE WRITING ON THE WALL

The God of Heaven predicted through Daniel, that Nebuchadnezzar, King of Babylon (the "Head of Gold") should be driven from men, and "thy dwelling shall be with the beasts of the field, and they shall make thee to eat grass like oxen...till thou know that the most High ruleth in the kingdom of men, and giveth it to whomsoever He will" (Daniel 4:25).

So if the God of Heaven delivered the "three young men" who trusted Him from the burning fiery furnace, and delivered Daniel from the lion's den, and humbled Nebuchadnezzar the mighty King of Babylon, surely He will deliver His faithful servants from the puny dictators of this decadent Twentieth Century.

WEIGHED IN THE BALANCES

If the "Head of Gold," which represented Babylon, and the "breast and arms of silver," which represented the Second world-empire, Media and Persia, failed to compel the Jewish captives to worship the state or the kings of Babylon, then surely those "two toes" out of the "ten toes" of Nebuchadnezzar's vision – the unspeakable Bolshevist and Nazi dictators – as the Bible predicted, can never unite against the Living God. Thus saith the Lord: "They shall not cleave one to another, even as iron is not mixed with clay" (Daniel 2:43). And where the "Head of Gold" failed, there is no chance for the "insignificant little toes" to succeed; and we can say of them, as Daniel said to Belshazzar: "And thou, his son, O Belshazzar, hast not humbled thine heart, though thou knewest all this; but hast lifted up thyself against the Lord of Heaven" (Daniel 5:22-23).

Therefore, the verdict given of Belshazzar was "God hath numbered thy kingdom, and finished it...thou art weighed in "the balances, and art found wanting" (Daniel 5:26-27), and – believe it or not – God has given a similar prediction through the College regarding Hitler, who has put people in prison because they did not worship himself and the State before God. Likewise, the same thing will happen to the other dictators unless they take warning from the downfall of Hitler and the Nazi régime, which is imminent.

The Penllergaer Mansion, 1938, from the West-side elevation. The main drive was 1 ¼ miles long, lined with rhododendrons and azaleas (at the opposite end of the building, out of view). It was the Bible College of Wales' fourth Estate in Britain and consisted of 270 acres.

CHAPTER 2

Three Remarkable Predictions

Among the many predictions made by the Bible College of Wales since it was started with the sum of two shillings only [£6.74 in 2020], are three outstanding ones.

They were: a prediction of a gift of £10,000, [£674,400 in 2020] another that God would give the offer of the Gospel to Every Creature in the ensuing thirty years, and that there would be No (General) European War during that time. Because these predictions were unique and apparently impossible of fulfilment they were eagerly seized upon by many of the newspapers, including the London dailies, and given wide publicity. By the Welsh Press the predictions were also given great prominence. The news-bills mention them in large type. As the man in the street read them he rubbed his eyes in more than mild surprise. Here are some of the news-bills relating to the predictions:

1. Swansea £10,000 Gift Prophecy Comes True. (28th July, 1938).
2. Swansea Bible College Chief and His "No War Prediction." (30th September, 1938).
3. Swansea Bible College Chief's New Prophecy On War. (11th September, 1939).

From an article in the Swansea *Evening Post* of July 22nd, 1938, the following is taken:

There are rejoicings at the Bible College of Wales, Derwen Fawr, Swansea, that the College's first £10,000 gift, the coming of which was predicted at the last Conference [Every Creature Conference] – has been paid into the College Bank Account.

An article in the *Western Mail* of July 23rd, 1938, stated:

£10,000 GIFT PROPHECY COMES TRUE. The Bible College of Wales, whose reliance on Faith to produce money to carry on its manifold activities is widely known, has just received its first gift of £10,000. This donation was predicted at a College Conference some time ago, and the Director, the Rev. Rees Howells, believes that it will be the first of many such gifts to be received.

Those who earn say four pounds a week know that it would take them fifty years to earn ten thousand pounds. If they could live on two pounds a week it would take them (not allowing for compound interest) a hundred years to save ten thousand pounds. Consequently the man in the street is baffled when he hears that someone, who has only faith in his vision to support him, says that he has received from God his Father a substantial gift of not less than ten thousand pounds. It is natural for anyone, hearing that such a prediction had come true, to say: "Who would not serve so rich a Father?" And when the ordinary man reads on the news-bills, or in his newspaper, that one man has had faith enough in his Heavenly Father to draw from Him ten thousand pounds, a deeper impression is made upon him than if he had listened to ten thousand sermons.

Such a prediction, when fulfilled, rouses great interest and becomes the table talk of thousands. Though our pseudo-astrologers and our Spiritualists often attempt to interpret the future, with laughable results, the man in the street is not really carried away. He knows without being told that only God can foresee events. Occasionally through circumstances or knowledge of the past, men sometimes guess the future with a moderate degree of accuracy; but not very often. The greatest men of every generation have proved how hopelessly wrong they are whenever they have forecast the trend of world events. The man who has managed to make one good guess seldom if ever contrives to guess right twice in a lifetime. Yet it has been done time and again by the Founders of the Bible College of Wales.

Whoever heard of a person foreseeing with absolute certainty that he was going to have a gift of ten thousand pounds from some person or persons unknown? Surely the man who dares foretell such an absurdity will get himself ridiculed; he will certainly get nobody to believe him, no newspaper to publish what he says, or to display it on its news-bills. That is unless his prediction has come to pass – as did ours of the impending gift of ten thousand pounds.

Guessing and hoping and feeling that a thing is going to happen can never produce that state of certainty that comes to one when God draws aside the curtain of fate, and allows His servant to get a vision of the future. Prediction, substantiated by the event, has more than once elevated the prophet to a position of high authority in the land. Two such men were both taken as captives to foreign countries, and these two – Joseph and Daniel – were each raised to the position of Governor or Viceroy in the country of his compulsory adoption.

For what reason? For predicting the future. Yet both testified that predicting the future was the province of God. Said Daniel: "There is a God in Heaven that revealeth secrets, and maketh known what shall be in the latter days" (Daniel 2:28).

After years in prison, suffering under a false charge, what else in this world could have raised Joseph in one day to be the ruler of Egypt save the fact that he was able to foretell the seven plenteous years followed by the seven years of famine? To those who did not understand, here was a mere slave ruling Egypt. Yet when Joseph interpreted his dream Pharaoh saw not a slave but "a man in whom the Spirit of God is" (Genesis 41:38). What a difference!

And so, for eighty years Joseph taught the senators of Egypt wisdom. And he showed both wisdom and the love which comes from God alone when he said to his trembling brothers who had sold him to slavery: "Be not angry with yourselves that ye sold me hither, for God did send me before you to preserve life. Tell my father that God hath made me lord of all Egypt!" (Genesis 45:5-9). What a man! What a brother! What a son! What a message to take to an aged father! And this because there is a God in Heaven who revealeth secrets!

Are those days of the open vision gone forever? Surely not. They are with us again today. For God still opens the future to His chosen servants. To the Bible College of Wales, through whom a number of predictions have been made already, God has more than once opened the future, as this simple narrative attempts to show. If the College remains obedient to His leading the open vision should be seen again and yet again.

THE "EVERY CREATURE" VISION

Five years ago there was given to the Director of the College a remarkable Vision. It foretold:
1. That God would give the offer of the Gospel to Every Creature during the next thirty years.
2. That God would call forth Ten Thousand people who would believe the Vision, and would send them out as His Witnesses unto the uttermost parts of the earth.
3. That God would open His Treasury to finance the Vision – the first gift to be £10,000.

Great Christian leaders of the last generation, men like J. Hudson Taylor, John R. Mott, A. B. Simpson and others, preached the possibility of Evangelising the World in their generation. But not one of them could say like Moses that God had commissioned him to do this great thing, or, had given him a sign as He did Moses, "And thou shalt say to Pharaoh thus saith the Lord, Israel is my son, even my firstborn…and if thou refuse to let him go, behold I will slay thy son, even thy firstborn" (Exodus 4:22-23).

When Pharaoh drove Moses and Aaron out of his presence, and set task-masters over the children of Israel, Moses was already aware, for God had told him so in Midian that the time was coming when He would slay his firstborn. And though by sending the frogs, flies, hailstorms, locusts and darkness, etc., God failed to induce Pharaoh to let Israel go, yet Moses knew that this last and most drastic sign, this killing of the firstborn would make Pharaoh thrust them forth – and so Pharaoh did.

As the slaying of the firstborn was a sign to Moses, so God's promised gift of £10,000 was a sign to the College which announced its coming beforehand, though yet unaware who was the donor-to-be. When the prophecy was fulfilled, it was felt to be a confirmation and, a sign to all that the College Vision was of God and neither man nor Devil would be allowed to hinder God from putting it through.

All interested in the evangelisation of the world know by experience that this can never be accomplished in their generation unless they receive a bigger blessing and greater power than was conferred on Christian leaders who lived before them, men like Martin Luther, William Carey, David Livingstone, D. L. Moody, and William Booth. Nearly two thousand years have passed since the Risen Lord gave the Command: "Go ye into all the world and preach the Gospel to Every Creature" (Mark 16:15), and yet not a third of this world has had the offer of salvation. So no existing organisation, striving its utmost, can do in thirty years what other excellent organisations, controlled by splendid Christians, have failed to do in two thousand years. But, when God gave the Vision to the College He also said: "I am coming down to do it," even as He said to Moses in Midian: "I am come down to deliver them out of the hands of the Egyptians?" (Exodus 3:8).

Even as Moses was given signs that he had been commissioned, so were the Founders [Rees and Lizzie Howells] of the College given signs with their commission, and one of the signs was the fulfilled prophecy of the Gift of £10,000 [£674,400 in 2020].

NO EUROPEAN WAR

Although the College has had numerous other gifts of as much as £500 a time, and ten single gifts of £1,000 a time, yet this special gift of £10,000 was different. And that is the reason why it is so much stressed in this volume. It was to be a *sign*, a *special sign* and a confirmation that the College Vision of the Gospel to Every Creature in thirty years was of God, and that God the Holy Ghost would put it through. In the days of Samuel the Word of God was precious because there was no open vision. "Where there is no vision the people perish" (Proverbs 29:18).

It is doubtful whether there has been really open vision since the days of Martin Luther. Through Luther God brought about the Reformation[1] [1517] when countries were changed and delivered from the yoke of Rome [Roman Catholic Church] into the glorious liberty of the children of God through believing that – 'THE JUST SHALL LIVE BY FAITH' (Romans 1:17).

We believe that the College Vision is a further maturing of the Promise God gave through the Prophet Joel: "In the last days, saith God, I will pour out of my Spirit upon all flesh" (Joel 2:28-29) – Every Creature! So then, this country is being prepared for an epoch-making event.

Through the fulfilment of one prophecy – the prediction of £10,000 – it is being prepared to take from God, another prophecy, one that will startle the world, that there will be "No (General) European War for thirty years."[2]

The £10,000 Gift concerned only the College. It was a sign that God wanted to give to those who had received and believed the College Vision. But this wider prediction of "No European War" is one that concerns the whole world, especially the Continent of Europe. Yet this prophecy was being repeated when it seemed that a *General* European War had already broken out! Nevertheless, the One who gave the Vision, and confirmed it with the gift of £10,000 has also made it known to us, that the bawling boastful dictators of Europe, can never make a General European War. The manner in which God made known this prophecy will be described in the next chapter.

CHAPTER 3

The Munich Prediction

After the arrival of the £10,000 [£674,400 in 2020] the next great test of the College Vision was the threat of a General European War. How could Every Creature be reached with the Gospel in thirty years, and how could ten thousand young people be trained and sent out as witnesses to the Lord unto the uttermost parts of the earth if a war like that of 1914 [to 1918] were repeated? For in the event of war, all the young people of military age would be called up, and College properties would be taken over for hospitals, etc. The 1914 war lasted four years, nearly every country in Europe was involved and millions were killed, but as Lord Baldwin told us, the next war would end civilisation!

In March 1936, just fifteen months after the College Vision was given Hitler marched his troops into the Rhineland. [A large demilitarised buffer zone inside Germany, which bordered parts of France, Belgium and the Netherlands. After WWI (1914-1918) it was occupied according to the Treaty of Versailles (signed at on 28 June 1919), with French and Allied troops, but as a gesture of good will they withdrew from 1926-1930]. He [Hitler] defied Britain and France, and the Treaty of Versailles and many expected France to defend the Treaty by declaring war on Germany. Then Britain, Italy and the other countries of Europe would have been drawn into war; and the Devil would have defeated God's plan of giving the Gospel to Every Creature in this generation.

The policy and propaganda of the Third Reich, the Nazi Government, were first to abolish trade unions and other organisations among the working classes. The German Pacifist Movement was also put down, anti-war publications were banned, and a nation of sixty million people were carried away with the slogan, "Peace with Armaments." The Press was soon muzzled; it became the mouthpiece of the Government, and journalists became political soldiers of Hitler. Education was also reorganised on the basis of "a nation in arms," military instruction was systematically given in schools, and the school teacher became a drill-sergeant. In an address to German teachers, Rust, the Prussian Minister of Education, said: "Gentlemen, you are the Storm Troop leaders of German education."

"REVEREND" STORM-TROOPERS

The only church that received Government support was the church that supported national defence as conceived by the Nazis. The right of the church to exist was only recognised so far as it agreed with Hitler's teaching. The Prussian Press Service even announced that many of the young pastors of their churches had been asked to be allowed to join the Storm Troops. But in the Evangelical churches resisters were harried and arrested; those who entertained unapproved ideas disappeared without being brought to trial; numbers were placed in concentration camps, where they saw and endured many horrors. So the pastor, who would escape persecution, had to be a spiritual storm-trooper, the school teacher an educational drill-sergeant, and the journalist a soldier with a lying pen.

Under the new Prussianised laws of Germany, criticism of the Nazi doctrine, their policy of "guns before butter" was equivalent to treason. For the first time in Germany, the land of the Reformation, freedom of thought, freedom of expression and freedom of worship were forbidden. Those who resisted were persecuted; the spirit of Antichrist was imposed on one of the greatest Protestant countries in Europe. So God led the College to pray against Hitler and the Nazi régime.

PRAYER AGAINST HITLER

During the crisis in March 1936, lectures and everything else were put on one side, and the College was given up to days of prayer and fasting. The conflict, "was not against flesh and blood but against principalities, against powers, against the rulers of the darkness of this world" (Ephesians 6:12). For three whole weeks over one hundred and twenty young people [largely students of the Bible College], who had been called to the Vision, *prayed until they prevailed with God to avert a European War.* On Sunday, 29th March 1936, they all made a vow to God that they would give their lives on the Altar, for God to use them to extend His Kingdom and give the Gospel to Every Creature; as really as they would have given their lives to their King and Country if war had broken out and they had been called up to the Western Front.

Those outside the College will never realise what those three weeks cost to about one hundred and twenty students and staff in order to prevail with God. These young people dedicated

- 37 -

themselves in a most active and practical sense to the College Vision. They "presented their bodies a living sacrifice, holy, acceptable unto God" (Romans 12:1). What individuals had done in other generations (William Carey for India, David Livingstone for Africa, and J. Hudson Taylor for China), a whole company of young men and women now did for all the nations of the world.

RUMOURS – NOT WARS

As soon as the College prevailed with God and came through to victory, God spoke through His Word: "Ye shall hear of wars and rumours of wars, see that ye be not troubled, for all these things must come to pass, but the end is not yet.... This Gospel of the Kingdom shall be preached in all the world for *a witness unto all nations*, and then shall the end come" (Matthew 24:6, 14).

From that day on there has been nothing but wars and rumours of wars; but not one of those who offered themselves as intercessors at that time has ever been troubled. The College Vision is based on the Word of God: "This Gospel...shall be preached...for a witness unto all nations, and then shall the end come," and the Saviour will return to reign for the Thousand Years. So the prophecy of "No European War" was the result of the three weeks of intercession in the College, and a message from the Word of God. It was clearly seen then and predicted that *all the dictators in Europe could never make a European War –* until the Vision was fulfilled. At that fervent time the second Psalm became a great reality in the College: "The kings (dictators) of the earth set themselves, and the rulers take counsel together against the Lord.... He that sitteth in the heavens shall laugh; the Lord shall have them in derision" (Psalm 2:2, 4).

God said to His Son: "Ask of me and I shall give Thee the heathen for thine inheritance, and the uttermosts parts of the earth for Thy possession" (Psalm 2:8).

From 29th March 1936 – the end of the three weeks of prayer – the Bible College of Wales became a new spiritual force. From henceforth we knew we could prevail upon God to keep His hand upon Hitler and his Storm Troopers, and prevent them from causing a general European War. So every time that Hitler made a new swoop, such as that on Austria, the College set aside days for prayer, to prevail upon God to prevent a war which, while bringing hell on earth, would hinder the College Vision from being put through in thirty years. Every time the enemy challenged the democracies and the Vision, all those who had dedicated themselves by a covenant of sacrifice, were as soldiers marching to the field of battle.

THE DARKEST HOUR

When the Munich clash came in September 1938, we knew that Hitler would not make a European War. In the darkest hour, when bloody conflict seemed inescapable, world leaders of religion – the Archbishop of Canterbury, the Pope and the Chief Rabbi – called for a Day of Prayer for Sunday, 18th September. But God had previously told the College to call for a *Day of Praise,* because they had prayed through to victory. And so the public Opening Day of the Session was one of Praise and Thanksgiving. The following excerpt from the "South Wales Evening Post" of 17th September 1938, is illuminating:

THE BIBLE COLLEGE OF WALES
OPENING of the First Term of the FIFTEENTH SESSION
THURSDAY, 22nd SEPTEMBER 1938.
Meetings at 3pm and 6pm.
THANKSGIVING AND PRAISE

The Meetings will take the form of Praise and Thanksgiving because God has again averted, a European War. The College belief and prophecy is that there will be no European War for the next Twenty-Eight years, until the College Vision of reaching Every Creature with the Gospel will be accomplished.

And what a day of praise it was – hundreds gathered in the Conference Hall [on the Derwen Fawr Estate] in the darkest hour thanking God beforehand, that there was not going to be a European War! The Lord then told the Director to do, as Jeremiah had done, send the prediction out to the country in writing, and let the millions hear it! So an article was sent to the "Evening Post" and the "Western Mail," and, on 29th September, the day before the Munich Pact was signed, a general holiday was given to the College and Schools. The same afternoon, a gift of £500 [£33,720 in 2020] was received at the College from an unexpected donor. It came direct from our Heavenly Father, because of our obedience in making the prediction known.

At the time when war seemed certain, a week before the Munich Pact, on 23rd September 1938, the "Western Mail" published the following noteworthy statement.

HE PREDICTS NO EUROPEAN WAR FOR THIRTY YEARS
DIRECTOR OF BIBLE COLLEGE TELLS OF VISION

Saying that he had had a Vision whereby the Gospel would be given to Every Creature within 30 years, the Rev. Rees Howells, Director of the Bible College of Wales, predicted at a meeting on Thursday that there would be no European War until the Vision was accomplished. The meeting was one of "thanksgiving to God for *averting a war over the Czechoslovakia dispute.*"

The following is from a further article which appeared in the "Western Mail" on 30th September 1938.

BIBLE COLLEGE CHIEF'S "NO WAR"
PREDICTION FOLLOWED BY GIFT OF £500

There was also a very great joy in the Bible College of Wales when the news came over the wireless (Hitler had invited Mr Chamberlain to meet him again), and at the same time the Director opened a letter with a gift of £500.

SLEEPLESS NIGHTS

The world at large will never realise what it cost the Director to obey God by committing himself and the College Vision, and making it known through the Press that there would be no European War while there was not one chance in a thousand to escape war. The Director had more than one sleepless night before he committed himself to the public through the *Western Mail* that there was going to be no European War, and the reason why God pressed upon him to do it was because of the hundreds of thousands of mothers who would break their hearts to see their sons going to be slaughtered on the battlefield....

Picture those fearful days, and picture the man in the street, who had probably read of the £10,000 prophecy and its fulfilment, now reading on the placards of the leading newspapers the further prediction of "No European War." For this latter prediction was not only displayed on the news-bills of the "Evening Post" and the "Western Mail," but also on those of the "Daily Mail" and other London newspapers, which, following the great publicity given to it by the local press, had also been impressed by the prophecy. People read it in Germany, Italy, and even in the Holy Land.

Sent out in the darkest hour of the crisis, the prediction became the subject of discussion among all classes of people, Members of Parliament, dockyard workers, and busy housewives, too. After the fulfilment of the prophecy and the signing of the Munich Pact, the Director was congratulated by all classes.

COLLEGE JUBILATION

The Director, be it remembered, had established the College, Schools, Hospital and other branches of the work, without any committee, council or denomination, looking only to God to guide and provide for everything. And people began to say that the man who could bring into being an institution representing in capital value over £100,000 [£6,744,000 in 2020] and who could rely on his God for a sum of £10,000 in one gift, was a receptive channel for the revelation of God's will. His other predictions must be worthy of attention.

When the general holiday was given to all branches of the College the day before the Munich Pact was signed, over two hundred day children from the Schools alone, went home to tell their parents that there was to be no War; one of the most striking of lessons in faith that could be given either to children or parents. Photographers from town came down to the College, and photographed an assembly of over five hundred people. The daily papers who had previously announced the prediction now published the photograph of the fulfilment jubilation. It was a triumph of faith in the God who is a Revealer of secrets. Thus a prediction in which the great nations of the modern world were directly concerned, a prophecy reminiscent of those mighty prophecies of the Bible, was fulfilled. It was, we repeat, given as a sign that God is going to give The Gospel to Every Creature in this Generation.

In the next chapter it will be shown how another Prediction, that concerning "Danzig and the Corridor" also triumphantly survived the great test.

The Munich Prediction College Jubilation with Glynderwen House in the background. 29 September 1938. The Munich Pact was signed the following day and war was averted, giving Britain time to re-arm.

CHAPTER 4

The Danzig Prediction

The greatest menace of 1939 was the conflict over Danzig and the Corridor, which Hitler had pledged himself to annex. Moreover, if he failed to acquire them as he acquired Austria and Czechoslovakia, he intended to take them by force of arms. As Poland had two million trained soldiers, and their bravery, shown in repulsing the Russian Army from Warsaw in 1920, was known all over the world, it was thought they would be able to withstand an attack by Germany, and carry on a war, at any rate for many months.

Britain and France had pledged themselves to the Poles, to defend Poland if Germany attacked her. It was understood, on the other hand, that Italy, Spain, and Japan would stand with Germany against Britain and France, if these countries should declare war on Germany. It seemed certain, therefore, that when Germany attacked Poland, nothing in the world could prevent a General European War. But the College had predicted that there would be "No European War" until the Vision of taking "the Gospel to Every Creature in thirty years" was accomplished; and then the real Armageddon would be fought. So sure were we of the prediction of "No General European War" that, after the September victory, when we gave a holiday before the Munich Pact was signed, the College was then led to buy one of the finest properties in South Wales, the [Penllergaer] estate of the late Sir John Llewelyn, and prepare for fruitful years of peace.

Meanwhile, Hitler, finding that the crisis created over Czechoslovakia did not lead to a European War (because Britain and France allowed him to have his own way), turned his wrath on the Jewish people, and caused thousands of their little children to become homeless (the number has been given as seventy thousand). The sufferings were so great, that the parents were even willing to give their children away, rather than see them starve.[1]

THE REASON BECOMES CLEAR

Thus it came about that God revealed to the College that they were to take over Sir John Llewelyn's Penllergaer estate, and make there a home and schools for Jewish children. (This will be explained in a later chapter). During 1939 the College spent thousands of pounds in making all preparations to receive the refugees while at the same time, waiting for the Danzig question to lead up to another crisis.

Germany under Hitler, like the Assyrian army under Sennacherib had never been checked nor defeated, and so was now like a roaring lion after its prey. German generals were visiting Italy, Spain, and other countries discussing war; and British generals were over in France, Poland, and Russia, making plans to combat the raging aggressor. Europe was preparing for the greatest war in history!

The responsibility and the tension of the prediction of "No European War," in face of the preparations for it, were so intense at times, that there was neither rest nor peace, except in the "cleft of the rock" (Exodus 33:22) and "under the shadow of the Almighty" (Psalm 91:1). Scores of times the Director [Rees Howells] made it known in the meetings, that when God confounded the dictators, it would be the greatest miracle of the ages, because only thus would a European War be avoided. More than once, when the dictators were rampaging over the wireless as to what they were going to do when the final test came, God had to comfort us, as He did Jeremiah, saying: "Behold, I am the Lord, the God of all flesh, is there anything too hard for Me?" (Jeremiah 32:27).

Was it possible for God to break the Axis, that diabolical union that the Devil had made between these dictators? Yes, the God who came down and confounded the tongues of those who were building the Tower of Babel, would easily be able to confound the plans of the puny dictators of 1939.

WAS IT OF GOD?

During the past seventeen years, God has led the College to make many predictions, some of which are given in this book. It has gained many thousands of followers and supporters, who for years have offered sacrificial gifts, as they were moved by God to do so. Last year alone, nearly £20,000 [£1,348,800 in 2020] was thus received. The fact that he had spent years in building up a work of this kind, and held properties in his hands to the value of about £150,000 [£10,116,000 in 2020], was in itself enough to make the Director very careful in all his predictions, because one real mistake would cause hundreds of supporters to lose their confidence in him. He knew well that the crisis over Danzig and the Corridor, would be the final test of the prediction of "No European War." So – was it of God or of man? Was God able to confuse the plans of the dictators, who appeared to be as firmly united and forged together as were Britain and France?

The College had staked its all on the God of Daniel, in whose hands even the great King Nebuchadnezzar found that "All the inhabitants of the earth are reputed as nothing: and He doeth according to His will in the army of Heaven, and among the inhabitants of the earth, and none can stay His hand, or say unto Him, what doest thou?" (Daniel 4:35).

When the clash came and Germany invaded Poland, some may have doubted. But the first ray of God's light was soon apparent, showing that God was surely working out the prediction.

ITALY AVERTS HER GAZE

After all her protestations of undying friendship, Italy and her dictator backed out. Incredible but true. Spain and Japan also declared their neutrality. In other words God broke asunder the Devil's league, and no power of evil in this world could bring the dictators together again. Mutual trust between the Axis powers was finally shattered. So God had confused the plans of the dictators! What a day of victory for the Bible College! The prediction had been vindicated. No general European War! Not until God permits the Armageddon. Victory beyond value. Although Britain and France, to carry out their pledge to Poland, declared war on Germany, the College knew that so long as Italy and Spain remained neutral, this would never lead to a general European War. When Germany made a league with Russia it was confirmed that both Italy and Spain would remain neutral. The Catholic countries have the greatest respect for their religion and their Sabbath, and they would never join Russia, who had done away with the Sabbath, even bringing her own pagan calendar into Poland.

To those who have eyes to see and ears to hear this joining up of Russia and Germany is a miracle, for they were the two most unlikely countries in the world to make a league with one another. Evil was designed, but here again God overruled it. The greatest enemies of the Nazis were the Reds, as Hitler has repeatedly said. But, just as Daniel made known, after he had seen the great image, whose feet and toes were part of iron and part of clay that "They shall not cleave one to another, even as iron is not mixed with clay" (Daniel 2:43), even so has it been with the four dictators in the day of battle, and so will it be with the Nazis and the Reds.

DISCOMFITED DICTATORS

The three great powers (Germany, Italy, and Japan), who had joined together under the cloak of an anti-Comintern pact, [Comintern was an international association of Communist parties, established in 1919] to work for a world war against Soviet Russia, posed as champions against Bolshevism. Hitler in one of his speeches, said: "The rulers of Russia today are blood-stained common malefactors, and the scum of humanity, who, favoured by the circumstances of a tragic hour, over-ran a great state, butchered and wiped out in wild blood-lust millions of their intellectual classes, and have now for years been exercising the most cruel tyranny in history. Nor let us forget that these rulers belong to a people in whom is combined to a degree seldom attained, bestial cruelty with unique fluency of lying, and which today more than ever believes itself called to the destined extension of its bloody tyranny over the whole world.... One cannot conclude any treaty with a partner whose sole interest is one's own destruction."

Germany, under the cloak of a crusader against Communist menace, was forging the Berlin-Rome-Tokio Axis, and claiming East Europe, as far as the Ukraine and the old Prussian colonisation areas leaving Italy to demand Tunis, Algiers, [in North Africa] etc., and Japan to do as she would in China. By making a pact with Soviet Russia, "the scum of humanity," as he called them, Hitler, to quote another writer, "broke the Humpty-Dumpty Axis beyond mending, and he can never put Humpty-Dumpty together again!"

AN AMAZING BREAK-UP

When it was predicted, through the College, that the Devil, through all the dictators of Europe cannot make a European War, God had already foreseen this. Russia only came in to take all the spoil from Germany, and then settled down to remain neutral. [Vyacheslav] Molotoff [Commissioner for Foreign Affairs] affirmed Russian neutrality by saying: "No one can draw Russia into war." No one but the Almighty God could have planned this amazing break-up, and have made it known before-hand.

Britain and France have become one in motive and aim, like parts of a living organism; but the league between Russia and Germany is merely an organisation, a union they try to make outwardly, when inwardly there is nothing but fear and enmity. So, from the day war was declared, and God proved the weakness of the dictators, the College saw that the prediction of "No European War" was safe; and it will shine more and more as the days and years go by, and the Vision is made known in every country of the world.

Yes, this confusion of the dictators is one of the greatest proofs that the College Vision is of God, and that He will give the Gospel to Every Creature in the next twenty-five years.[2]

"Sing ye to the Lord, for He hath triumphed gloriously" (Exodus 15:1).

> Blessed and glorious King,
> To Thee our praise we bring,
> This glorious hour....
> *War now has vanquished been,
> Dictators all are seen –
> Ne'er to unite again.
> Due to Thy power.[3]

*European War.

Editor's note: The above hymn and many others can be found in: *Rees Howells, Vision Hymns of Spiritual Warfare & Intercessory Declarations: World War II Songs of Victory, Intercession, Praise and Worship, Israel and the Every Creature Commission* by Mathew Backholer, autumn 2021. A collection of rare hymns and choruses from the Bible College of Wales under Rees Howells' Directorship spanning the pivotal years of 1939-1948 and brought to life for the first time in more than seventy years. Fully annotated and featuring a number of rare photos, poems and letters.

CHAPTER 5

The Great Prediction

God Will Intervene To End Hitler's War

When Hitler in 1933, became Chancellor, he became like Haman of old, the Jews' enemy. As Haman did, he appointed a day (1st April) to make a national boycott against the Jews. It was probably the greatest act of folly ever committed on April Fool's Day, for the Nazi Brown Shirts began to show the dragon's teeth which are destined to grind them to pieces. The world's press termed this blended violence and mendacity "Nazi savagery against Judah." The excesses committed then and since have shocked civilisation profoundly. Jewish doctors born in Germany were dismissed from public service, teachers from their schools, and lawyers from the Law Courts. Business houses were induced to dismiss Jews from their staff, and Germans were forbidden to buy in Jewish shops. Mobs ran amok, robbing Jewish stores, and committing acts of brutal ferocity; and the police did not intervene to restrain the terrorists.

Hitler, aware that the nations of the world were disgusted with his régime, defied humanity, declaring there was no cruelty in thus purging the German nation of an alien and a *Criminal Race,* which had brought ruin on Aryan Germany. The behaviour of the fanatical despot, not only shocked the civilised world, but assuredly shocked God as well. Hitler's treatment of the Jews, and his reference to them as a *Criminal Race,* could not escape the notice of Him who inhabiteth eternity and weighs all acts of men in His balances.

When Balak sent for Balaam he said: "Come, curse me Jacob, and come, defy Israel" (Numbers 23:7), and Balaam said: "How shall I curse whom God has not cursed? Or how shall I defy, whom the Lord has not defied? Surely there is no enchantment against Jacob, neither is there any divination against Israel" (Numbers 23:8, 21). "I shall see Him, but not now; I shall behold Him, but not nigh: there shall come a *Star out of Jacob,* and a Sceptre shall rise out of Israel" (Numbers 24:17).

It would have been well for Hitler had he been guided by that saying from the history of the people he blasphemously branded as a *Criminal Race.* Compare the prophets of the Gentiles, who have lived during the last two thousand years, since the Day of Pentecost (the Dispensation of Grace) with those of the Jews who lived for two thousand years before Pentecost (back to the time of Abraham). Is there one among the Gentiles who can be put alongside of Joseph, Moses, Elijah, or Daniel?

Even Martin Luther saw only the truth of "Justification by Faith," which the Apostles experienced and preached; but Luther did none of the miracles that Peter and Paul did; nor has any other Gentile ever repeated any of the Acts of the Apostles, such mighty works as the calling of Dorcas back from the dead, opening of the prison doors, etc., etc.

HISTORY WARNS HITLER

We dare not treat lightly God's promises to the Jews – His Chosen Race. God's Covenant with Abraham was: "…I will multiply thy seed as the stars of Heaven…and in thy seed shall possess the gate of his enemies; and in thy seed shall all the nations of the earth be blessed" (Genesis 12:2-3 and 22:17-18).

Israel was to be a blessing to the world, but let him who offends the Chosen Race – beware! Though God allowed two nations, Egypt and Babylon, to chastise Israel, He did not thereby endorse all the ways of those nations. Rather did He bring those nations into His judgment and they were overthrown. How then can Hitler, who persecuted the Jews without cause, hope to escape the fate which befalls those who lift up their hands against the Lord's anointed? God said to Abraham: "Thy seed shall be a stranger in a land that is not theirs, and shall serve them; and they shall afflict them four hundred years; and also that nation, whom they shall serve, will I judge" (Genesis 15:13-14). And in Egypt God fulfilled that prediction to the letter – not only killing the firstborn, but drowning Pharaoh and his army in the Red Sea. To this day Egypt is but a third-rate nation.

Again God said to Jeremiah: "These nations shall serve the King of Babylon seventy years. And it shall come to pass, when seventy years are accomplished, that I will punish the King of Babylon, and that nation. I will bring upon that land all My words which I have pronounced against it. I will recompense them according to their deeds…" (Jeremiah 25:11-14). So shall it be with the Nazis. The Lord has made known to the College that He is going to destroy Hitler and the Nazi régime, and the College has predicted it beforehand through the Daily Press, that the world may know that it was God, and God alone who scattered the dictators, and bound the Devil that he could never unite them to fight side by side against God and the right.

God isolated Germany, and caused to go against her, England and France, who have repeatedly said that they are not fighting against Germany as a nation, but against Hitler and the Nazi régime, and they will not make peace with Hitlerism. After our prediction had gone out to the country, there came the Prime Minister's reply to the Hitler peace proposal. Speaking on behalf of the Empire, Mr Chamberlain said: "We unitedly reject it." He added that it would be impossible to make peace with the present German government, for Hitler and his Nazis could never be trusted again.

It was on Saturday, 9th September, and Monday, 11th September, 1939, in the columns of the "South Wales Evening Post," and the "Western Mail," that our new prediction was first published. The article from the "Western Mail" is given here in full:

GOD WILL INTERVENE TO END THE WAR[1]
WELSH BIBLE COLLEGE DIRECTOR'S PREDICTION

Very soon God will intervene in a miraculous way and come to the aid of England and France, who have sacrificed all to defend liberty, especially religious liberty, and put down the Antichrist which has thrown its spell over Germany and caused all the outstanding evangelical ministers to be put in prison and concentration camps.

This is the view expressed by the Rev. Rees Howells, hon. director of the Bible College of Wales, Swansea; in a circular he has issued dealing with the international situation.

Mr Howells continues: "Although England and France have declared war on Germany to carry out their pledges to Poland, God has kept out the German allies – Italy, Spain, and Japan – who before the crisis were as much in league with Germany as France and England were in league with Poland, and through another mysterious way Russia, at the last moment, became neutral.

"So after a week of hostilities, and after a week of prayer and waiting upon God in the College, it is now clearer than ever to us in the College that the prediction of "No European War" is from God, and that He has isolated Germany so that He may get at this system of the Nazi régime, which is the AntiChrist, and release Germany, 'the land of the Reformation.'

"WILL DEAL WITH NAZI RÉGIME"

"The College for weeks and months prayed this prayer three-and-a-half years ago, and we firmly believe now that God will answer that prayer; that God will intervene in a miraculous way just now, and will deal with Germany as he dealt with the Egyptian Army in the time of Moses and with the Philistines in the time of the Prophet Samuel when he raised his Ebenezer.

"We are stronger than ever in the belief that God is in this crisis, and that God has singled out Germany to deal with the Nazi régime (Hitlerism), which is the Antichrist, which would be the greatest opposition to the College Vision of giving the Gospel to Every Creature, because this system of the Nazi régime has caused the best of the evangelical ministers to be put in prison.

"DEADLY BLOW TO HITLERISM"

"Moreover, no missionaries would ever be able to go from Germany as the Moravians[2] of old did, and before this war will go much further God will intervene in a direct way and put this system down, and end the war, and release Germany, the land of the Reformation. He will deal a deadly blow to Hitlerism, and the prediction of "No European War" will stand out clearer than ever. Our Prime Minister will soon see the day when his hopes of peace, instead of being shattered, will become true in Europe again."

The College believe, adds Mr Howells, that God allowed England and France to go to the aid of Poland so as to hold Hitlerism in check, and that God will cause Hitler to fall on the battlefield, or by a mutiny, or a great rising in Germany against the Nazis. The words of David regarding King Saul will soon become true: "The Lord shall surely smite him; or his day shall come to die; or he shall descend into battle, and perish" (1 Samuel 26:10).

It was on 12th September, the day following the publication in the "Western Mail" of the foregoing article that our Prime Minister made it known to the world that "this country can never again accept terms of peace coming from Hitler or the Nazi régime."

So, after a month of hostilities, when the offer of peace came, the world waited and watched to see whether the Prime Minister would go back on his word or not. Thousands of leaflets were published by the "Peace Pledge Union," calling for peace and a conference. But, because of the prediction of "the downfall of Hitler and the Nazi régime," the College was bound to stand with the Prime Minister in stating that the war must be continued "until Hitlerism is overthrown."

BRITAIN ON GOD'S SIDE

History will show that the College stood firmly with the Prime Minister in 1938, when he was inspired to go direct to Hitler, and avert a European War; for *Mr Chamberlain was acting in accordance with the prophecy*. When some people blamed the Prime Minister for flying to Germany, saying that by taking things into his own hands, he had broken every law of diplomacy, the Premier's answer was: "*I am man of peace,* and war to me is a nightmare." There was no other way to avert war, and save millions of lives, and he would follow the same course again. But a year later, in October 1939, the College was confident that God guided Britain and France to refuse Hitler's peace proposal; even though, like so many more, the College had much to lose by the continuance of war. For, we repeat, the Founders are now holding in trust for God, freehold properties to the value of £150,000 [£10,116,000 in 2020], as well as that which is infinitely more valuable than property – the Vision of giving the "*Gospel to Every Creature in thirty years,*" with which is linked the prediction of "No European War" during that period.

If Italy, Spain, and Turkey had joined Germany and made it a *general* European War that would have belied [contradicted] the College Vision. But God isolated Germany, so as to get at this Nazi system, which is the Antichrist, and give it a death-blow. For it is His will to release Germany, the land of the Reformation, and to release the land of the Moravians, that hundreds of missionaries may again be called out of both countries to share in the Vision of giving the Gospel to *Every Creature* in this generation.

How often of late has the College been encouraged to believe in its own Vision by reading the story of Isaiah's prophecy about the Assyrians, who came down like a wolf, like Hitler today. The College prediction is like that of Isaiah, who predicted of that great boaster, King Sennacherib, that God would put a hook in

- 52 -

his nose, and a bridle in his lips, and turn him back-and that night, God smote in the camp of the Assyrians 185,000 people (Isaiah 36-37).

Was there not ample reason for God also to intervene against the Nazis? Into what a state our country has been brought! For over a year people have had to keep gas-masks to hand. And now, through fear of air-raids, the King and Queen, down to the lonely peasant and his wife in the remotest parts of the country, have to take their gas-masks with them in case of poison gas from the air. Everywhere death is threatened.

Hitler boasts that he will destroy the one thing he fears most – the British Empire. He can never do it. If Britain and France were to make peace with Hitler and the Nazi régime, people would have to keep their gas-masks indefinitely, so long as the Nazi Government existed. For, as we have said, they could never be trusted not to break out again. Because our new prediction will be fulfilled, and "God will intervene in a miraculous way," our nation must now hasten to turn back to God, must keep her Sabbaths yet again, according to the Fourth Commandment, and must restore the old Puritan England of the past. In short, we must now build Jerusalem in England's green and pleasant land,[3] which was the Vision of the late King George the Fifth.

ARMAGEDDON

All who have read the book "Hitler Re-arms" – which is an exposure of Germany's War plans – will praise God as long as they live, that He has isolated Germany, and divided the dictators, who would otherwise have plunged Europe and the world into the bloodiest war in history. All their preparations for war, their guns and bombs, their poison-words and poison-gas have given millions of people a taste of what the coming Armageddon will be like. But then, alas, God will not intervene, as He is going to do now, by bringing about the speedy downfall of the Nazi régime.

The Bible has predicted the world conditions that will precede the Master's "*Second Coming*." The two great *signs* are:

1. "And ye shall hear of wars and rumours of wars, see that ye be not troubled, for all these things must come to pass, but the end is not yet. This Gospel of the Kingdom shall be preached in all the world for a witness unto all nations; and then shall the end come" (Matthew 24:6, 14).

2. The Jews will return to the Holy Land. "The Land of Promise." "Then the Lord thy God will turn thy captivity, and

have compassion upon thee, and will return and gather thee from all the nations, whither the Lord thy God hath scattered thee" (Deuteronomy 30:3).

The College Vision is that the Gospel will be given to all nations in the next twenty-five years (for five years have already gone since it was received), and then – the Prince of Peace will come to reign on the Earth. Even so come Lord Jesus!

The next chapter records the prediction that God would make a Home for the children of the Jewish refugees, to educate and train them and send them back to the Holy Land to wait for the Lord's Coming.

CHAPTER 6

The £100,000 Prediction

Homes For Jewish Children In
Wales And The Holy Land

Yet another remarkable prediction, given to the College, has been confidently noised abroad, though as yet it has only been partially fulfilled. It is that God will send £100,000 to the College to be used for the benefit of Jewish refugee children. The College, believing that this £100,000 will arrive in due course, has evolved a scheme which will operate on the Barnardo [a children's charity] principle. The main features of this scheme are as follow:

1. No destitute refugee child to be refused, but promptly admitted.

2. The children are to have a home and education until they qualify as teachers, nurses or missionaries.

3. There will be no distinction made between Christian and orthodox Jewish children, if the parents or guardians will trust their upbringing to the College.

The following is an article which appeared in the "Western Mail" on 29th May 1939, when the persecution was at its height, in which the prediction and scheme are explained more fully:

£100,000 EXPECTED BY BIBLE COLLEGE

NEW SCHOOLS FOR 1,000 JEWISH
REFUGEE CHILDREN

Two prophecies are made in the report of the Bible College of Wales, Swansea, to be presented at the fifteenth annual meeting today. They are: 1. "That the Lord will give the College during the coming year £100,000," and 2. That schools will be built to take in between 1,000 and 2,000 Jewish refugee children so that they may have four years' training in the Secondary Schools and three in the Bible College.

The report states that just as "the £100,000 gift from God's treasury" and the prediction of no European War were made known in the last annual report and by now had been fulfilled, so in the present report the Holy Ghost was making the two further prophecies known.

It is also prophesied that God will again keep back a European War until the College Vision of reaching Every Creature with the Gospel will be accomplished and homes established in the Holy Land for hundreds of Jewish refugees.

PENLLERGAER BOUGHT

Since the crisis last September, says the report, the College has been buying estates on which to build schools for the Jewish children: 1. Twenty-one acres of freehold land adjoining the Bible College estates were taken over last September. 2. Penllergaer, the estate of the late Sir John Llewelyn, has been bought. This estate is of 270 acres. "All this land has been bought so that God may fulfil His promise to give the College £100,000 to be used for the refugee Children." Each refugee child will cost at a minimum £1 a week because those who adopt them must sign that they will be responsible for their education, clothing, food, and a home until they are 18 years of age. Therefore, in addition to the thousands of pounds which the new schools, colleges, and hospital will cost, 1,000 Jewish children will cost £1,000 a week (£50,000 a year).

£50,000 GUARANTEE NECESSARY

"The College," says the report, "will have no claim upon any source for a penny towards maintenance of these children but on God, who has promised to be a father to the fatherless. Since the College bought these 21 acres near Derwen Fawr and the estate of the late Sir John Llewelyn a law has been passed that with each adopted refugee child there must be a bank guarantee given of £50 [£3,250 in 2020] for those up to 16 and £100 for those over 16. Therefore, by taking 1,000 Jewish children the College will have to guarantee £50,000, this money to be used for their migration to another country. So the Holy Ghost has foreseen that the College would need £100,000 for buildings and bank guarantee besides the £50,000 per year which will be needed for the maintenance of the children in this country.

The Bible College after 15 years in Glyn Derwen [the first site bought in 1924 and originally spelt as two words but later contracted to one word: Glynderwen] and Derwen Fawr will move to its new home, Penllergaer, shortly. In the College today are students of many nationalities, including Russian and Spanish refugees, Jewish refugees, and a Prince of Abyssinia [Ethiopia].

£360 A WEEK IN GIFTS

The money that came in gifts last year was more than three times greater than the money received in College and School fees. The financial report shows that there was received in gifts alone £18,771, [£1,266,000 in 2020] an average of £360 [£24,346 in 2020] a week. One gift alone was for £10,000 [£674,400 in 2020]. All the money was received "through prayer alone." From fees £5,327 [£359,260 in 2020 from the College, Schools, Hospital, Home of Rest for Missionaries] was received, so that the total receipts amounted to £24,101 [£1,625,400 in 2020].

"Here is a College," states the report, "which was founded on 2s [£6.74 in 2020], without a committee, council, or denomination or any appeal being made in any shape or form, with a turnover of £24,000 for last year, and most of that money has come from outside Wales and nearly all of it spent in the borough of Swansea."

The founders of the College (the Rev. and Mrs Rees Howells) have decided to give their home in Derwen Fawr for use as a Girls' Secondary School and Glyn Derwen as a Boys' Secondary School in order that Derwen Fawr, Sketty Isaf, and Glyn Derwen may be devoted entirely to the refugees. The director is inviting Lord and Lady Baldwin to open Penllergaer because of their great interest in Jewish refugee children.

CITY OF REFUGE

Our new Home for the Jews is an estate of nearly three hundred acres of freehold land; it has a large mansion with many outbuildings; and the latter are being reconstructed to provide lecture-halls and class-rooms, and fifty additional bedrooms. There are seven other dwelling-houses on the estate, a home farm, and the market gardens where Sir John Llewelyn once employed fifteen gardeners. The estate is famous for its collection of trees and shrubs, which is one of the best in the country; it was here that the Swansea University used to send their students for classes in botany, before the town built their Educational Gardens.

The river and the lake of eighteen acres have long been popular for their trout fishing, and round them are the lovely woods where Sir John entertained shooting parties. The beautiful drive up to the mansion, through masses of rhododendrons and azaleas is over a mile-and-a-quarter in length. When the persecuted little ones are driven up through these banks of rhododendrons, ablaze with bloom, they will feel they are more than half way already to their Home of Destiny, the Land of Promise, which is yet again to flow with milk and honey. This then is the estate on which it is purposed to establish a "City of Refuge" in Wales for Jewish refugee children, where they may "flee from the slayer."

The evidence already apparent that God Himself has planned and led us to take in hand a schemes such as this, has increased our conviction that He will send in the hundreds of thousands of pounds that will be needed to establish a "City of Refuge," not only in Wales, but also in the Holy Land and elsewhere. It also buttresses our belief that He will intervene to prevent a general European War and to smash the diabolical Nazi régime.

Remembrance of recent horrors may help people to realise something of the feelings of God, who is a "Father of the fatherless," when He called the Founders of the College to launch out on this colossal scheme. In Britain, thousands of little children have been evacuated from London and other great cities [from 1st September 1939], for protection against air-raids, and from such a disaster as overtook the mothers and children of Warsaw [in Poland], where over twenty thousand civilians were killed in a few weeks. Over seventy thousand helpless refugee children need homes, education and protection. Will the fathers and mothers of our country pray that all these will have homes, even as our own children had when they were evacuated from our cities?

We give here the photograph of our first Jewish baby, who came to us from Vienna, with several other children, when he was just a year old. Like Moses, found in his ark of bulrushes on the banks of the Nile, and subsequently brought up in a palace, so little Herbert Grunhut[1] travelled here in a tiny basket to be cared for like an infant prince in one of his Father's earthly mansions.

Herbert "Bert" Grunhut (1938-2019) from Vienna, Austria with Lizzie and Rees Howells in front of Derwen Fawr Mansion 1939

FAITH'S GOLDEN RULE

There is a golden rule in the life of faith, that the Christian can never prevail upon God to move others to give larger sums of money towards God's work, than he himself has either given, or proved that he is willing to give if it were in his power to do so. The rule applies to a Bible College as well as to an ordinary Christian. It came within the power of the Founders of the College to offer to God the first £100,000 towards establishing the "Cities of Refuge" in Wales and the Holy Land, and so that offering was made, although it would have meant selling up all that they had.

When the Conscription Bill [3rd September 1939] was passed and the young manhood [aged 18-41] of our country was mobilised, the Government bought the freehold land adjoining the College [on Derwen Fawr Road, Sketty, Swansea]. On this they began to erect large buildings for the use of the Territorials and the new Militia Army, [later known as the Home Guard] and there was the possibility of their needing all the College properties.

These were very suitable for Government purposes, because they included a Hospital, Laboratory, Gymnasium and Bakery; and by adapting some of the class-rooms and lecture-halls room could have been made to billet a thousand men.

It was even suggested that when the Government decided to take over the three estates [Glynderwen, Derwen Fawr and Sketty Isaf] that the College should have the honorary chaplainship. The College had already bought Penllergaer [six miles north of the three other estates], where there is room to build a town of about two thousand houses. So it was settled that if the Government should decide to take over our College with the fifty acres of freehold land surrounding it, we would move all our work out to Penllergaer, and there begin to build on faith again Colleges, Schools, Missionary Home, Hospital, Bakery, etc., which would cost over £100,000.

There would then be no money or realisable [gain or profit] property for rebuilding, because the £100,000 or so raised from the sale of the properties would be dedicated to the "Cities of Refuge" for the Jewish children. In other words we were prepared to make an offering to God of £100,000 – the value of our College property – for helping the children of His Chosen People. Because we were prepared to do this, we were observing a rule of faith whereby we might confidently look to God for an equal sum for our genuine needs. Prayer was made to God to allow us to use this £100,000 realisable on College property in this way. However, at the last moment, the Government decided not to take any more land in our neighbourhood, as the War Office wrote to us: "The military authorities in the Western Command have, however, been asked whether they wish to acquire any of these properties for any other purpose. As soon as a report is received Mr Hore-Belisha [British Secretary of State for War 1937-1940] will write to you further."

So the Lord allowed us to retain the estates on which the College stands, Glyn Derwen and Derwen Fawr; the former to be continued as a Boys' Secondary School, and the latter to established as a Girls' Secondary School, but College itself will be moved to Penllergaer.

Thus the path is now clear for the Lord to make the College the needed gift of £100,000. We have not a shadow of doubt that the money will come, or that the vision of its coming will be fulfilled. God has said in Psalm 68: "A father of the fatherless, and a judge of the widows, is God in His holy habitation. God setteth the *solitary in families*, He bringeth out those which are bound in chains."

When God made this Promise to be a Father to the fatherless, He bound Himself to be more of a Father to the orphans than the father and mother they had lost, and by becoming their father, He pledges Himself to provide for them. The Word of God says: "If ye then, being evil, know how to give good gifts unto children, *how much more* shall your Heavenly Father" (Matthew 7:11). If He told us to consider the ravens and the lilies, and He feeds and clothes, *how much more* will He feed and clothe these children?

THE SOLITARY IN FAMILIES

Dr. Barnardo (1845-1905) had a revelation of God to set the Solitary in Families, and so he built the Girl's Village Home, and rescued, clothed, fed, mothered and educated over nine thousand girls in one village alone.

Although he died at the age of sixty, he rescued, during his lifetime, over *sixty thousand orphans*. Since Dr. Barnardo, by becoming a channel through whom God could fulfil His Promise to the Orphans, rescued sixty thousand in thirty years, the Lord can, and the College believes will, through then, rescue fifty thousand little Jewish children in twenty-five years. What a company to meet the Saviour in the Holy Land at His Second coming as their Messiah, The Prince of Peace.[2]

Through the Prophet Isaiah God gave a special promise to the orphaned Jewish Children: "Thus saith the Lord God, behold, I will lift up Mine hand to the Gentiles, and set up My standard to the people, and they shall bring thy sons in their arms, and thy daughters shall be carried upon their shoulders. And kings shall be thy nursing fathers, and their queens thy nursing mothers.... Shall the prey be taken from the mighty, or the lawful captive delivered. Thus saith the Lord, even the captives of the mighty shall be taken away, and the prey of the terrible shall be delivered: for I will contend with him (Hitler) that contendeth with thee, *and will save thy Children*" (Isaiah 49:22-25).[3]

GOD'S GREAT DELIVERANCE

Let us look again at Hitler, this time in Rome. Only in May 1938, when Hitler visited Rome, and Mussolini Berlin, Hitler stressed "Colossal unity of Germany" with Mussolini saying "So long as the united community with its front to the world, *nobody will war on us.*" And Mussolini said: "No one can weaken the Berlin-Rome Axis. The friendship between the two countries is everlasting."

"Everlasting" was hardly appropriate. "Ephemeral" was surely the word for an Axis that lasted hardly a year. Yet Mussolini – at the time of the Hitler visit – spoke on racial purity, and opened a campaign against the Jews; he also imposed military training upon all boys from the age of eight until they entered the army, and at the same time he took steps to strengthen the Italian Fleet. Just then it really looked as though nothing could save the world from the dictators. They seemed invincible. Yet the break-up has come and gone, and little has so far been said about it. The world will never fully realise how great is God's deliverance from these ruthless dictators, men whom the Devil would have used to plunge the world into the bloodiest war in history, and for the slaughter of many millions of people.

Already we breathe more freely again. And although the struggle may be great, the sun will again shine in the heavens upon the democracies who will come to understand that they were all the time fighting on the Lord's side, while but feebly hoping that the Lord was with them, and so would enable them to overthrow their powerful enemy. This strange war then is not our war, but God's, and the victory is the Lord's.

The best thank-offering that we can give to God for deliverance from black-outs and gas-masks, from shot, shell and explosion, is to succour these little helpless Jewish children, innocent victims of the Devil's violence, whose despairing parents are willing to give them to the Gentiles, rather than see them perish exposure, bestial cruelty and starvation, and help them we can and will. Thus we shall help God to fulfil His Promise "I will save the Children" (Isaiah 49:25). Thus we shall earn the welcome benediction: "Inasmuch as have done it unto the least of these…ye done it unto Me" (Matthew 25:40).

PART II

CHAPTER 7

Prediction of the Largest Bible College

Nowadays there is a great scarcity of mighty men of faith. For this reason it was difficult seventeen years ago to convince the country of the prediction to build the largest Bible College by prayer and faith alone, especially as it was our first great prediction.[1]

Of the millions of Christians in our country in the last generation there was only one, a German named George Müller, who, trusted God, and God alone, to supply hundreds of thousands of pounds to carry on a work that God had committed to him. George Müller was the outstanding man of God who never looked to man, who made no deputation work of any kind, although his needs ran up to £90 a day. Consequently only George Müller and the Old Testament Prophets were able to supply the Founders of the College with the necessary examples to trust God alone day by day to supply the financial needs for this monumental work.

In August 1922, without any seeking on the part of the Founders, God revealed to them that it was His will and purpose to build a large Bible College in Wales, to be founded, and sustained by prayer and faith alone. The idea therefore originated with God, without premeditation or even desire on the part of the Founders.

It would seem that in our time God wanted to give another visible proof that He is the living God, and that we can still rely on His Word and His promises. So the College was to be without a committee, council, or denomination; it would spring up with no visible support of any kind, no human patron, no endowment.

God wanted to prove that faith and prayer, are efficient agents, along with implicit trust in His Word for meeting all needs. He wanted to raise up a College to be a testimony to the world that God's work carried on by the Holy Ghost, needs not the patronage of the world; and that God's work, carried on in God's way, will never lack finance, because God is the Owner of all "the silver and the gold" (Haggai 2:8).

The call to build a College on Faith came quite unexpectedly. The Founders were on furlough from Africa, where, for nearly ten years (1914-1923)[2] they had laboured as missionaries with the South African General Mission. During two fruitful years of this period they had travelled over 11,000 miles conducting special meetings round all their Mission stations in South Africa. It was directly after this most successful period of their missionary work that God's call came to remain at home and build the largest Bible and Missionary Training College in the country. Why the largest? Time will show. Anyway, the call was clear and definite. Judge the work by its fruits. Already there has been harvest. But there are plenteous harvests yet to come.

MONEY MIRACLES

Surely one of the most fascinating of tasks is to trace back a story of God in His faithfulness, searching out His Almighty power and wisdom in fulfilling a promise made to one of His servants to whom He has given a commission to undertake beyond his range and power.

When God inspired the building of this College, by faith alone, He gave two promises.

1. "Fear not…He will not fail thee, nor forsake thee, until thou hast finished all the work for the service of the house of the Lord (the College). "There shall be with thee 'of workmanship' every willing skilful man, for any manner of service" (1 Chronicles 28:20-21).

2. The promise of "A Talent of Gold" (Exodus 25:39, the figure given then was £6,150) [£374,600 in 2020].

As already stated, when the call came from God to buy estates on which to build the largest Bible College in the country, the Founders had only two shillings. [The cost of a 1939 *God Challenges the Dictators'* hardback]. So from a human standpoint, without a council or any visible support during the greatest period of commercial scarcity of money in history of the country (1920s), it appeared to be a hazardous and even a crazy venture. It was a time when, through financial and strain in the business world, banks and men's heart's everywhere failed them. It would therefore seem that the call came to build the College of Faith at that time so as, among other things, to encourage businessmen to trust in God, because a living trusting faith in God is above all circumstances.

No delays can discourage faith, no loss of friends or depression in trade can touch it; faith goes on its steady course, and triumphs over all difficulties. That is one reason why it is so necessary to stress that the only thing on earth to fear is – *estrangement from God.*

THE FIRST PURCHASE

The first estate bought by faith for the College was Glyn Derwen, the home of Mr Charles Eden, an uncle of the Right Hon. Anthony Eden, where in past years Mr Eden must have spent many a happy holiday. This estate, with its large mansion, comprised many acres of land, and incidentally a public-house.

The property had been laid out in lawns, tennis-courts and gardens, allowing a commanding view of Swansea Bay and the Mumbles. Since, during the summer months, visitors pass it daily to the Gower Coast, it would also seem that God had planned this College of Faith to be a silent witness to multitudes of passers-by of what He will do in answer to believing prayer.

Like some of the others, this property, which cost over £6,000 was bought when there was hardly a penny in hand. Yet on the morning of the day when the deposit had to be paid, three cheques came in from some distance away and from unknown people. One of the cheques was for £126 [£7,630 in 2020], and the three together brought the amount in hand up to the last shilling required for the deposit!

This was our first convincing victory in finance; in an unmistakable way God showed what He was able to do, and what He would do in the future, if we looked to Him alone. "Let your requests be known unto God…. My God shall supply all your need" (Philippians 4:6, 19).

OUR PUBLIC-HOUSE

The next few months [of 1923] were spent alone with God, learning further how to prevail on Him to move His stewards to send the thousands of pounds needed to complete the prophecy. During those stern days of waiting and learning in the School of Faith, an offer came to buy from us the public-house and the four acres of land attached to it. *No new licence had been given in Swansea for many years, so the licence itself was worth over a thousand pounds, and acceptance of the offer to buy the public-house would supply the extra money needed to complete the first purchase of the property.* It was the first serious temptation, in finance, to take an easy way of deliverance.

Days were spent waiting upon God in prayer to find His will regarding the selling of the public-house, but there was no possibility of compromise on principle. The unequivocal answer came: "Trust ye in the Lord for ever, for in the Lord Jehovah are everlasting resources" (Isaiah 26:4).

So the offer to trade the public-house and thus to have an easy deliverance for the purchase of the property was politely turned down. Instead, the public-house was closed down and the value of the licence completely lost. But the licensee was compensated for clearing out. Fair is fair to all – saints and publican alike. Then, by the addition of eight rooms, the public-house itself was converted-into a men's hostel!

Thus the second victory was gained; and God, as a reward for our faith and trust, sent in many hundreds of pounds in large and small gifts. When completion of purchase was made, it was found that the price, with costs, amounted to £6,150 7s. 4d. The very amount that God had promised! What a wonderful God to serve!

GOD'S COLLEGE

The College was dedicated on Whit-Monday, [Pentecost-Monday, 9th June] 1924, and hundreds gathered in the grounds for the special service. Long articles, describing the unique event were published in the daily Press, especially in the "Daily Leader," and the Welsh National newspaper, "The Western Mail." The Press head-lines read:

BIBLE COLLEGE OF WALES
A TRIUMPH OF FAITH
FERVENT INAUGURATION

The Press called it "God's College" – a happy title.

God had indeed given the College, for the funds had come from Him. God had stirred the hearts of His stewards to give freely, and so what was done in the Dedication Service was but reverently to hand the College back to God's care. He had given it, and it was given back to Him; the Founders would continue to look to Him to take care of His own, and were confident that He was going to do it.

Thus was founded the largest College of its kind in the country, with, at one time, more than one hundred and forty students in residence. In the first seven years, the Lord sent in thousands of pounds and supplied our needs day by day. Deliverances repeatedly came in at the very hour of need, and urgent needs for the next meal were frequently met only after the last meal had been cleaned away.

But space will not allow of full details to be given; it is only desired to show here how the prediction of building the largest Bible College in the country by prayer and faith alone was fulfilled; that it is now an accomplished fact, and that the evidence is there for all to see. This College has already been a blessing to thousands of people, especially as an incentive to faith in God in all times of distress and financial difficulties.

HALF FEES FOR STUDENTS

Hundreds of students have passed through the College to different parts of the Mission Field – young men and women who because of lack of funds, could never have taken a three years' course – had not the College opened its doors to them, and provided training, board and residence at less than half the actual cost. Students were only required to find the first £10 [£610 in 2020, for one term's fees of which there were three terms per year] and then to enter the School of Faith, there to learn, during three years' residence, to change God's promises into current coin [a phrase popular with Rees Howells]. Many are now missionaries in the foreign field. So again a fulfilled prediction made us raise our Ebenezer: "Hitherto hath the Lord helped us" (1 Samuel 7:12).

After some years of learning in the School of Faith and Prayer at the new College, God called us to further advance by making known that we were to buy Derwen Fawr, the estate of Sir Charles Ruthen. How this new marvel was accomplished will appear in the next chapter.

CHAPTER 8

Prediction of Buying Derwen Fawr

God had told the Founders to buy Derwen Fawr, the Estate of the late Sir Charles Ruthen, who had been Director of Housing for the Ministry of Health. This Estate was famous, for among its guests had been Mr Lloyd George (and family) when he was Prime Minister, Lord Melchett (Sir Alfred Mond), and other Cabinet Ministers. It had also been the home of members of the well-known Richardson family. Sir Charles had spent thousands of pounds on the Estate, buying all the land between Derwen Fawr Road and Mumbles Road to prevent any buildings being put up in front of Derwen Fawr. Thousands of pounds had also been spent on laying out acres of land in lawns and gardens; and Sir Charles had displayed great architectural skill in altering the mansion, and in making the beautiful Italian gardens, for which he had costly stone-work brought from Italy.

When this estate came to the market, it included seventeen acres of freehold land in the best part of Swansea. Every acre could be turned into building land, for the town was moving down towards Singleton Park and the University; and soon afterwards the Swansea Corporation [local Council], having bought Sketty Park Estate, built their fine Civic Buildings near Singleton.

A TILT WITH ROME

When the Lord revealed [in 1929] that we were to buy Derwen Fawr Estate, the Director found that the Church of Rome were already negotiating for it. It was against the same Church that the College had previously to fight when they bought Glyn Derwen. To make known beforehand, while still without money, that God, through the College, would again oppose the Church of Rome, and a Syndicate also in the field, and would buy Derwen Fawr, at a time when the country was in a state of financial embarrassment, was surely a most daring exploit of faith.

The purchase of Derwen Fawr with no money and against double odds was as much in the impossible as that other unlikely prediction that there would be no general European War. The natural man can never understand these predictions with his unenlightened reason; for they are not in the realm of reason, but in the realm of Faith, which is the realm of God. The Master said: "When He, the Spirit of Truth, is come, He will guide you into all truth…and He will show you things to come" (John 16:13). As we have said, it was the Holy Ghost Himself who made known beforehand that Glyn Derwen should be bought, and a Bible College built there by faith. Again it was the Holy Ghost who said beforehand, and had the prediction made known, that the College should buy Derwen Fawr Estate, even against such great opposition.

At the time the negotiations were going on, a few thousand leaflets were published [the exact number was 4,000] making the prediction known to the public. The conflict lasted for months. There were days of tension when it was touch and go between the College and the Syndicate, for Derwen Fawr was one of the most desired and desirable building estates in Swansea. The only claim we had on Derwen Fawr was that some months before, Lady Ruthen had promised the refusal of it to the College. When the sale of the property was put in the hands of Lady Ruthen's solicitor, who did not know of this promise to the College, he was naturally on the side of the highest bidder, the Syndicate, which had made a slightly higher offer than the College.

None of us will ever forget the day when the depressing news came that Derwen Fawr had been sold to the Syndicate. We brought it before God, asking why He had given the prediction and caused us to make it known all over the country that He was going to buy Derwen Fawr for Himself, seeing that He had permitted it to be sold to another? As a result, and against known facts, the College refused to believe that Derwen Fawr had been sold to the Syndicate.

OUR RED-LETTER DAY

The day of the climax is one which we shall long remember. It was a Monday morning, and the Director's cousin, a doctor in Swansea had gone with him to the solicitor's office, where the two heard from one of the clerks what seemed to be final, that "Derwen Fawr is sold." That was definite enough. The solicitor himself was ill in bed, but had phoned the message through. Now indeed was the prediction sorely tested. Was it really from God, or from man? If it was from God, Derwen Fawr could never be sold to another person. So sure was the Director that it was from God, that he then announced, "Derwen Fawr is not sold. God's Word can never fail!"

At once his cousin visited the solicitor at his home and stressed that the College was entitled to the estate, because it had been definitely promised the first refusal of it. It was then learned belatedly that the Syndicate had merely been given a promise of the estate, provided they closed with the offer on the morning that the solicitor was too ill to attend to the deal. As they had not been able to close, this opened the way for the College to come in on the promise previously made by Lady Ruthen, as it was rightly entitled to do. In other words, this prediction too, was fulfilled, because God had intervened at the last moment to honour His promise.

Even so, Derwen Fawr was also secured when there was not a single penny in hand to pay for it. Fortunately, the solicitor had only stipulated that the Director should go to his office next day, and put down £25 [£1,590 in 2020], which would suffice until he had time to make out a regular contract. Fortunately, too, that very day two gifts were received, one of £5 and the other of £20. So Derwen Fawr was bought by faith in just that simple, unflinching faith which achieved those stirring exploits recorded in the eleventh of Hebrews:

By Faith they passed through the Red Sea as by dry land.

By Faith the walls of Jericho fell down.

By Faith they subdued kingdoms…stopped the mouths of lions.

By Faith they quenched the violence of fire…turned to flight the armies of the aliens.

THE TRUE PROPHET

By simple faith God took these beautiful estates, erected handsome new buildings on them worth thousands of pounds, and so proves to the world that He is the same today as yesterday, and that He will repeat what He did yesterday through the Prophets, when He will find a man with faith equal to that of the Prophets. Today the word prophet has come to mean a preacher only. But the prophets of old predicted the future as well, God making known to them beforehand what He was going to do. So to the prophets the future was like the past to the historians.

But who can understand these things today? For "the natural man receiveth not the things of the Spirit of God, for they are foolishness unto him, neither can he know them, because they are spiritually discerned" (1 Corinthians 2:14).

The Saviour said: "I thank Thee O Father, Lord of Heaven and earth, because Thou hast hid these things from the wise and prudent and hast revealed them unto babes" (Luke 10:21).

In the next chapter we show how, by faith, which is foolishness to the world, we received from God those thousands of pounds required to pay for this new acquisition, the Derwen Fawr Estate.

Derwen Fawr Mansion, c.1934 with a small section of the Italian Gardens on view with the FAITH IS SUBSTANCE / JEHOVAH JIREH plinth on the right in white. The two-storey building on the left was an extension that Rees Howells added and upstairs was used as staff rooms. Downstairs was a small meeting hall with a piano and a pulpit and could accommodate around eighty people, more if they sat on the stairs.

CHAPTER 9

Money Like Manna

The title of this chapter was a sub-title to an article published by the "Evening Post" and the "Western Mail" to describe the buying of Derwen Fawr by faith. The article ran:

FAITH WORKS WONDERS FOR
SWANSEA BIBLE COLLEGE
MONEY LIKE MANNA

Blackpill Bible College[1] continues to present a spectacle of money pouring into a religious institution like manna from Heaven. Money coming in to the extent of thousands of pounds in spite of bad times. The College is one of the strongest and most impressive examples of faith manifested by works in modern religious history.

The supreme aim of the College was the glory of God. One step taken in faith and prayer always prepared for another; and each new experience of trusting God emboldened us to step out on a larger venture, proving that there was no risk in confidently leaning on the Word and faithfulness of God. So long as we were single-eyed to the glory of God, and the extension of His Kingdom, we could claim the promise: "All these things shall be added unto you" (Matthew 6:33), because "Your Father knoweth that ye have need of these things" (Matthew 6:32).

In leaning upon the living God for some years to supply every need, we proved that prevailing prayer was largely conditioned by constant obedience; so every new step had to be promptly taken in faith as soon as fresh leading was given. The largest amounts of money that God would have to provide, would still further prove to the watching world the power of prayer offered in faith.

When God commanded Moses to build the Tabernacle in the Wilderness, He also stirred the hearts of the people to bring in "free offerings every morning," so much so that the people had to be "restrained from bringing, for the stuff they had was sufficient...and too much" (Exodus 36:3-6).

Again, later, when David desired to build a House for the Lord, the people were so stirred that they brought in *princely* gifts until silver in Jerusalem became like stones for abundance. So, likewise, for years God had stirred the hearts of His stewards to give large gifts to the College. But from that time on we looked to Him to send *princely* gifts.

Advance steps in the Bible College were often taken when there was a lack rather than an abundance of money. At times, when needs were most pressing, God would suddenly call us to launch out on an undertaking that would involve thousands of pounds of additional expenditure; as in the buying of Derwen Fawr.

LARGE GIFTS – ON THE NAIL

As by faith we took the challenge to buy Derwen Fawr when we were without a penny, and the deposit had to be paid next day, our prayers were consequently much increased and our faith did not fail under the test; rather was it strengthened. And so, in three days we received five gifts: £250 [£15,900 in 2020], £300 [£19,080 in 2020], £50 [£3,180 in 2020], £25 [£1,590 in 2020] and £50. This abundantly enabled us to pay the sum required for the deposit, and so to secure legally the property for the Lord.

During the following month, among other gifts, there came in one of £400 [£25,460 in 2020] and another of £1,000 [£63,650 in 2020]; and each of these arrived on the very day the money was called for. When God is the deliverer, He frequently plans the supplies to arrive on the nail, the very day when they are needed.

What a shout of victory there was in the College when, after four days of waiting upon God in believing prayer the first gift of £1,000 came in! After that the College received no less than nine further gifts of £1,000 each; and though rejoicings followed the arrival of each £1,000 not one gave us the thrill of the first. We had imagined the joy of receiving the first thousand pounds, but imagination at best is as shadow to substance, in comparison with the real joy of receiving the actual cheque with the certain knowledge that it had come direct from our Heavenly Father.

The joy of such a large deliverance, meeting an urgent and essential need, must be experienced before it can be appreciated. In reading the Song of Moses, one can readily understand the feelings of the Patriarch, for it was the outcome of his own personal joy for the deliverance of his oppressed people from Egypt, and his exploit of faith in opening the Red Sea, and rolling it back upon the discomfited Egyptians.

Those who have not experienced great deliverances of faith, cannot know the joy of them, or how blessedly near they bring one to God; especially large deliverances such as gifts of £1,000 and £10,000. Receiving such bounty direct from the hand of our Heavenly Father, in the very nick of time, brings back the Word of the Master: "If ye then, being evil, know how to give good gifts unto your children, how much more...your Heavenly Father" (Matthew 7:11).

Think that while He meets the needs of millions who appeal to Him in their distress, He can also give, just to one of His children, who is extending His Kingdom, a *princely* gift of £10,000. Suppose His children all had faith, how rich God would have to be even to give £1,000 to each of them! But the Prophet said: "The silver is Mine and the gold is Mine, saith the Lord of Hosts" (Haggai 2:8), and while He is the Owner, our source of supply will never be exhausted. Such large gifts impress us with the Majesty of God. The sensation they give is like that experienced on visiting the Niagara Falls[2] for the first time; an overwhelming feeling of awe and reverence, for one is conscious of standing in the presence of the Great Father – Creator Himself.

FAITH WIELDS A TROWEL

While we were praying for the Derwen Fawr Estate, and still looking constantly to the Lord for the daily needs of the College, the fresh command came from God to: "Go forward and erect new buildings." The first two to be built were a College Chapel to seat two hundred [opened in January 1931], and a Conference Hall [completed in April 1931] to hold five hundred. Then came two men's hostels and afterwards a women's hostel to house over one hundred students in residence.

At the time when the workmen were engaged to start their labours, again there was not a penny in hand; but, although they were regularly employed for over eighteen months, entailing a weekly wage of between £30 [£1,910 in 2020] and £40 [£2,546 in 2020], not once did they go away without receiving their full pay. Even so, on Friday, it was a rare thing to have any money in hand for the Saturday's wages; and very often the Lord would allow the first post on a Saturday morning to go without the deliverances, so that we should have a time of prevailing prayer before the second post. Yet our loving Heavenly Father never once failed us, and every Saturday we were able to pay our workmen and to raise our Ebenezer, and gratefully proclaim: "Hitherto hath the Lord helped us" (1 Samuel 7:12).

"CHRISTIAN" SCEPTICS

Buildings worth thousands of pounds were erected on the new estate, proving daily that he who leans upon the living God alone, is beyond disappointment, for "No good thing will He withhold from them that walk uprightly" (Psalm 84:11). But even with such a monument of faith and these wonderful visible proofs, blind unbelief and jealousy even in ordinary Christians is sure to err; it will always attribute God's workings, however wonderful, to some natural means of influence; and, instead of giving the glory to God, will persist in explaining away the miracles of prayer and grace. In the sight of God it is surely almost blasphemy to attribute His work to some natural means, instead of rejoicing and praising God that the Holy Ghost has come again to do the "greater works" (John 14:12). Did they not say to the blind man: "Give God the praise: we know that this Man (the Lord) is a sinner" (John 9:24).

FAITH THROUGH DISCIPLINE

When Derwen Fawr Estate had been added to Glyn Derwen, and the College enlarged and re-opened [in 1930] on the two estates, there were over one hundred and thirty students in residence, but it was just as easy for God to carry the double burden, as it had been for Him to shoulder a single one. All that He asked of us was implicit faith in Him, then nothing would be impossible. As faith was constantly exercised it grew stronger still, so that it now became as easy to ask God for a thousand pounds, as it had been to ask for a hundred pounds ten years before.

Faith once strengthened through discipline, can never be made to doubt, however great the delays and testings.

The Word of God says that the trial of your faith is "much more precious than of gold that perisheth" (1 Peter 1:7). "Count it all joy when ye fall into divers testings...that ye may be perfect and entire, wanting nothing" (James 1:2-4).

The Saviour said: "Have faith in God. For...what things soever ye desire, when ye pray, believe that ye receive them, and ye shall have them" (Mark 11:22, 24). This has been the experience of the Bible College of Wales from its foundation, "and the half has never been told" (1 Kings 10:7).

Derwen Fawr Mansion c.1932. Behind this Mansion was Derwen Fawr Road and the Sketty Isaf Estate

CHAPTER 10

Prediction of a Third Estate

School for Missionary Children

The time soon came for yet another advance by faith. This new "push" would mean an outlay of some further thousands of pounds to buy a third estate, and to erect on it the requisite new buildings; also thousands of pounds more each year for upkeep. A large staff of "degree" men and women would be needed before the school could be recognised by the Board of Education. Without money or an influential supporting committee, no sane man would have undertaken such a gigantic scheme as buying an estate and erecting thereon buildings worth thousands of pounds to establish Preparatory and Secondary Schools, much less have undertaken to work the scheme out, unless his faith was unshakably fixed on an Almighty God, whose financial resources were unlimited. *Furthermore, no man could ever have been driven by such a self-seeking purpose to venture on such an impossible scheme.*

Only a conviction that he was doing the will of God could have prompted such an extraordinary action. So that, in the greatest test and the darkest hour, the Founder was always able to say: "I am following One who is leading me."

Again let us stress that the human impossibility of such an undertaking only served to reveal more clearly the wonderful hand of our Guide. A man, without money, in sole dependence upon God, able to add thousands of pounds a year to his, present great liabilities, was an unusual figure. He was bound to convince many ordinary men, as well as some eminent business men and financiers, that it is surely not a vain thing to trust in the living God; and these have not been backward in saying so.

And still, through the College and its branches, the Holy Ghost again says, as the Master once said: "I have greater witness than that of man, for the works which the Father hath done, the same works bear witness of Me" (John 5:36).

Verily God at work in Swansea for all to see!

GOD'S OVERFLOWING TREASURY

By now, through the witness of the daily Press, the attention of millions of people has been drawn to this Faith Monument, which is drawing thousands of pounds each year from God's Treasury. This last year (1939) gifts totalling nearly £20,000 [£1,348,000 in 2020] came in, proving once again without a doubt, that there is a living God in Heaven that rules in the affairs of men, who can easily move donors to send gifts both small and great.

Very often God moves the most unlikely people, just as He moved Cyrus, a heathen king, to provide means for the rebuilding of His temple. We are assured that this same God will yet provide millions of pounds for the College Vision, and so extend the offer of the Gospel to Every Creature.

At the time when God revealed His will to provide both Home and Education for the Missionaries' Children, the College began to negotiate with the Swansea Corporation for Sketty Park, but at the last moment the Corporation decided not to sell. However, just at that time the Dowager Lady Swansea died, and Sketty Hall became vacant. As Sketty Hall is a part of Singleton Park, and is so near the Swansea University, it would be a most convenient estate on which to build a large Secondary School; for after matriculating, the missionaries' children could go on to the University to study for their degrees, using Sketty Hall as their home, and so finishing their education under our care.

So the late Sir Percy Molyneux, who had often befriended us, appealed to his friend, Lord Swansea, to sell Sketty Hall to the Bible College of Wales, but the reply was that Sketty Hall was not in the market just then. Yet what a challenge of faith to bid for another estate worth thousands of pounds. Again, with an empty bank!

THE COST OF PROPHECY

Those who have never been called to believe and to prove God in the seemingly impossible, have no idea what the prophets of old went through, or what it cost a man like Moses, who had to look to God alone to provide for over two-and-a-half-millions of ungrateful people (the population of Wales) in a sun-baked wilderness. The man in the street, like certain scholars, does not believe in miracles; for no one in the present generation has been able to repeat them, or give any visible proof that God can do them today. Common-sense and reason say that if God is the same today as yesterday, then why does He not repeat Himself as the Great Miracle Worker?

The correspondence between Sir Percy Molyneux and Lord Swansea made it plain that Sketty Hall could not then be sold. But later, when the Swansea Corporation made an appeal for Sketty Hall, Lord Swansea wrote to Sir Percy saying that, as he felt indebted to the Town, and had been a member of its Council, the Swansea Corporation had the first claim on it; and so the Council are building a large Secondary School on the estate today.

Although unforeseen obstacles prevented the College from becoming the owners of Sketty Park or Sketty Hall, yet we always knew that all hindrances were under God's control; and that if He did not give this estate for the missionaries' children, it was because He was about to give a better or a more convenient one. Truly "He gives the very best to those who leave the choice to Him." At this time of launching out, another estate, Sketty Isaf, came onto the market. This was an estate of seventeen acres of freehold land adjoining the Bible College at Derwen Fawr, and the owners were willing to sell the house standing on it, with five acres only, and give the option of purchase on the other twelve acres at a later date. So the College bought Sketty Isaf with the five acres, and have since bought the other twelve, and also a still further seven acres of adjoining freehold land.

Since then the College has acquired Penllergaer, the 270 acre estate of the late Sir John Llewelyn. The details of the purchase are given in another chapter.

So instead of Sketty Park and Sketty Hall the Lord has given us Sketty Isaf and Penllergaer. When the prediction of *great extensions* was fulfilled by these important purchases there was again great joy in that College – the Bible College of Wales.

TENSION

The reader, even if he is not a business man, may realise what tension there is when negotiating for properties worth thousands of pounds. Imagine then the increased tension when habitually negotiating without money. Frequently it was touch and go for months. At any time we might be tempted to abandon an inspired vision of the future, because of the lack of so many thousands of pounds in the bank. Although God has said that He is the Owner of "the silver and the gold" (Haggai 2:8), and "the cattle on a thousand hills" (Psalm 50:10), and "all the fowls of the air are His," (Psalm 50:11), yet everyone knows that the money God needs may be invested in other things.

Often it takes time for His stewards to change their stocks and shares into hard cash, for few people have sums like £1,000 or £10,000 lying loose at their bank. That is why the College has always had to pray beforehand for the very sum that the donor will have to give. (Prayer went up daily for months for the gift of £10,000). The Lord has to move the donor first, and then the donor has to release his stocks and shares, or some other property. So there are many processes going on in the spiritual realm before Faith becomes Substance, and the prayer-warrior obtains visible evidence that his prayer is answered. Yet faith is still "the substance of things hoped for, the evidence of things not seen" (Hebrews 11:1). We know for God has proved it so.

LAWS OF GOD'S SUPPLY

Like everything else the life of faith has to be learned. It took George Müller nearly twelve years of living daily from hand to mouth before he learned it. Conditions had to be fulfilled; laws that neither the natural man nor the average intellectual man knows anything about, had to be inflexibly obeyed. It takes many years before a man can become as confident in a life of faith, as an ordinary business man is confident when he has a large surplus in the bank. To those who have never entered this School of Faith, the thought of trusting God and not a bank balance for money is indeed frightening. But as time passes and God proves again and again that He never faileth, fear changes to calm reliance. The Waves and the Winds beat upon the Rock of Faith but the Rock stands firm, serenely confident. For is it not the Rock of Ages?[1]

After seventeen years of laying foundations, and learning more and deeper lessons daily in the School of Faith our confidence in God has become unshakeable. We have branched out, without one anxious thought. We have opened a new Bible College in Paris [bought in January 1939] and expect to open more in many other countries, including the Holy Land and India.[2]

In the next chapter will be shown how the money came to establish the Secondary School, and how we received a still greater blessing. For, in answer to believing prayer there came to us the consecrated staff to run it. True indeed was the prediction that God would meet our urgent need by sending us the assistance of the servants of His choice.

The Glynderwen Estate with Glynderwen House at centre back c.1928, with classrooms and accommodation buildings. The two buildings in the distance (top right) were not part of the Bible College of Wales.

CHAPTER 11

God's Hundredfold

When God called Abraham to leave his country, his kindred, and his father's house, the Covenant He made was to bless him *and his seed:* and the Saviour gave the same promise to every missionary – "there is no man that hath left house…or father or mother, or wife *or children* for my sake and the Gospel's, but he shall receive a hundredfold, *now in this time*" (Mark 10:29-30). So if the missionary can leave his children because he believes that God will through him offer the Free Gift of Eternal Life to the heathen, surely he can believe that God will give the hundredfold more to his children, than to the children of the ordinary believer who has never left anything or anyone for the Gospel's sake.

When the Lord called the Founders to leave their only son, Samuel, who was not a year old, in order to become ambassadors of the Cross in Africa, they did as Hannah of old did with her Samuel – "lent him to the Lord as long as he liveth" (1 Samuel 1:28). So God became responsible to provide him a home, education and everything he needed;[1] and as the old coloured man in America said: "When God does a thing, He does it handsome." God gave their son the very best home, and provided for his schooling, and for three years in Oxford, where he graduated; he is today on the College staff, and is Deputy Director. The ordinary believer can never provide for his child as God can, and few of them have been able to send their sons to Oxford or Cambridge, as many missionaries have done, because it is God who provides the hundredfold.

God commanded the Founders to make a Home and Secondary School for Missionaries' children, as He commanded the widow woman of Sarepta / Zarephath to feed Elijah (1 Kings 17:9 and Luke 4:26). She only provided the first meal, for that was all she had: it was God that caused the barrel of meal and the cruse of oil not to fail until the rain came. The God who commanded to build the Schools was the One who gave the money for erecting new buildings and to maintain the staff. All the new buildings of the College have been built by direct labour, because God only provided by the day and by the week. So God had to give the plans to us in detail, as He did to Moses for the erection of the Tabernacle and to David for the building of the

Temple; and He also had to provide men like Bezaleel and Aholiab, "skilled in all manner of workmanship" (Exodus 31:2-6 and Exodus 35:30-35). In this way, new buildings worth over £30,000 [£2,022,000 in 2020] have been erected on the four estates.

THE WAGES OF FAITH

It was decided to turn Glyn Derwen [later contracted to a single word Glynderwen], the first estate, into a Secondary School, and the day came when the Lord said: "Arise and build." As usual there was not a penny in hand when the builders arrived; God did not deliver the money for their first week's wages until the second post on Saturday, when a cheque for £20 [£1,400 in 2020] came. The following Saturday, He did not deliver by post, but sent a donor to the College with £25 [£1,750 in 2020]. In a similar way He provided each Saturday for the first month. Then, one day, when money was required to pay for materials, and there was not a penny in hand, a cheque for £350 [£24,500 in 2020] was received. Again, one Monday, a day when gifts are not really expected, the three posts brought in three anonymous gifts, £100, [£7,000 in 2020] £50 [£3,500 in 2020], and £10 [£700 in 2020], from different parts of the country.

What object lessons these were to over a hundred young missionary students! Along with studying Greek, Hebrew, Theology and Church History, they were able to take part in prayers for money and to see God answering them in a direct way; and they agree that "an ounce of experience is better than a ton of theory" [a phrase popular with Rees Howells]. In a College of Faith like this, where the needs have to be provided for by the day or by the week, the students, after completing their three years' course, are able to say with the Apostles of old: "That which we have heard, which we have seen with our eyes...and our hands have handled, of the Word of life...declare we unto you" (1 John 1:1, 3).

Because this is a work of faith, the Lord has not allowed us to be slack in coming up to the requirements of the Educational Boards. Two residential buildings had to be erected for the staff and the missionaries' children; also nine class-rooms, a large gymnasium and the science laboratory. The work of building went on steadily for about two years, so that faith was kept in constant exercise to bring in the weekly wages, and provide thousands of pounds for materials. When the first £1,000

[£70,000 in 2020] came in towards the School, there was a great shout of victory, and another when the second £1,000 followed. God's hundredfold. Then, the beginning of August a third £1,000 was received, and before the end of the month still another £1,000 came in. August is usually regarded as a lean month, because many of those who have means are on their holidays, but − God never goes on holiday: "He that keepeth Israel shall neither slumber nor sleep" (Psalm 121:4). Thus God sent four gifts of £1,000 during that summer. All we could say was: "Blessed are those who put their trust in the living God." So, in answer to believing prayer, the Lord sent in all the money required to provide the necessary buildings for the School to be *recognised by the Cambridge Board [*July 1937].

GOD SENDS THE STAFF

As God had promised the hundredfold to the missionaries' children even in their education, He had to provide the very best staff for the School, and give each one a personal call to the work. As of old His promise was: "There shall be with thee for all manner of workmanship every willing skilful man, for any manner of service" (1 Chronicles 28:21). The first one called to the School staff [Miss Doris M. Ruscoe] had been a Senior Mistress in Matlock Secondary School for nine years. She came on a visit to the College, and received the College blessing, which has enabled every member of the staff to forsake all and follow the Nazarene − to be a disciple not only in word but in deed. Then the Head Master, [Mr Kenneth McDouall] who is a Cambridge man, and the son of a Missionary, after receiving the blessing, had the call and forsook all to follow the Master.

The Head Mistress [Miss Elaine Bodley] of the Preparatory School is an Oxford graduate who had honours in Modern Languages. [She joined the staff of the Bible College of Wales in 1931 and transferred to the Preparatory School in September 1934]. Others followed, so that by today there are over twenty on the Educational staff of the schools − without counting the Home side, men and women with some of the best degrees in the country, who are out-and-out for God, and have dedicated themselves in a most practical way to be fathers and mothers to the missionaries' children.

The School and the tutors have made such a name in the district that over two hundred children from the best homes in Swansea are attending as day scholars; and a large number of them have been converted in the School. So the Lord is raising up a new generation as He did with the Israelites in the wilderness, where all those who were under twenty when they left Egypt were taught by Moses. They became those faithful followers of Joshua, who walked like one man into the Jordan, and never flinched at the walls of Jericho. So the children who have been brought up in our Schools will be among the ten thousand picked men and women whom God will use to take the Gospel to Every Creature. God's ways are "past finding out" (Job 9:10 and Romans 11:33).

Sketty Isaf Mansion c.1932. The Bible College School began in this building with eleven children and two full-time teachers and one part-time teacher in September 1933. In 1935, the School had outgrown Sketty and moved to Glynderwen, less than five minute walk down the road towards Blackpill. The School was later renamed Emmanuel School, then Emmanuel Grammar School and included a Preparatory School which worked out of Sketty Isaf and Derwen Fawr.

The Schools belong to the Lord, and although they were recognised by the Cambridge Examinations Board a couple of years ago, we have not applied for any grant. This is open for us, as for the Catholic Schools, but we want the Lord to have the honour and glory of providing for His own School. Not only in the last Cambridge School Certificate Examination did the Bible College School have the average passes of the country, seventy percent, but also in the three exams, in the past two years.

No child whose parents have left their country for the Mission Field is to be refused admission; and the parents are only required to find half the actual cost of maintaining each child £30 [£2,100 in 2020] per annum for education, board and residence, holidays included.

Last year the College only received through fees from all sources (College, Schools, Conferences, etc.) a little over £5,000 [£337,200 in 2020], but the gifts from God were almost four times as much as that, nearly £20,000 [£1,348,800 in 2020].

Sketty Isaf Mansion 2011. The three-storey extension is on the left plus a *garage underneath (*out of view) and was built under Rees Howells. Sketty Isaf Mansion and out-buildings were demolished in 2015 and the Sketty Isaf Estate is now known as Howells Reach with fourteen houses with an average value of around £550,000 each.

BABIES' HOME

As God has promised to be a "Father to the fatherless" (Psalm 68:5), and especially to those whose parents have died in His service on the Mission Field, their children are to have a home and education in the College, and God, in answer to prayer, will provide the means of sustaining them. That is why the College has also established a "Babies' Home." The first orphans received were two little girls [Joan and Christina Partridge] whose parents had died in Central Africa, [Belgian Congo] and – whose last wish was that their children should have a home in the College. They came a few years ago, [1936] when the younger one was under twelve months old; both are in the School today, having a home and all their needs provided for by their Heavenly Father.

Because Dr. Barnardo put out that notice "No destitute child to be refused," God, through the Barnardo Homes, is providing today for a family of over eight thousand. So the Lord, through the College, is ready to provide a home and education for all those children whose parents have died on the Mission Field. The Lord has also purposed to build a Normal Training College, and a large Hospital on the new estate of Penllergaer; so that, after taking the Matriculation and School Higher, the missionaries' children will be able to complete their training, and qualify as teachers or nurses, and then go straight to the Mission Field.

The Schools, therefore, are great monuments of faith, and have already been a blessing to hundreds of homes including those of many of the day scholars. By the completion of the Schools we saw the fulfilment of another great prediction. And again we raised our Ebenezer, and sang another song, like the Song of Moses – a Song of Victory, for Him who commanded His thoughtless disciples to let the little ones come unto Him.[2]

CHAPTER 12

Prediction of Home And

Hospital For Missionaries

As we have emphasised already the promise that they will receive a hundredfold more in this present time applies to all missionaries who have left their homes for the Saviour's sake, and have taken the Gospel to foreign lands. Abraham, by stepping out in obedience to God, had thereby a claim on God to give him "the land of Canaan," and to make his seed as innumerable as "the stars of the heavens" (Genesis 22:17); for this was God's promise, and when Abraham believed it, "it was counted unto him for righteousness" (Romans 4:3).

Similarly, the missionary, *called* and *sent forth by God,* who has "forsaken all" (Luke 14:33) to answer the call; when he comes back to this country, has a claim on God to provide a home for him, for the Master promised him "the hundredfold" (Matthew 19:29). Because God promised Eternal Life as a gift to anyone who believes in His Son, the worst sinners, like the thief on the Cross or Jerry McAuley, who became the a Spirit-filled evangelist, can receive it.[1]

The moment they believe, God is honour bound to give them the gift of Eternal Life, and that only because He promised it. By merely believing God, millions have received this gift, and they:

"Shall never perish" (John 10:28).

"This is the record that God hath given to us Eternal Life, and this life is in His Son" (1 John 5:11).

"He that believeth on the Son *hath* Everlasting Life" (John 3:36).

Why is it that the same missionaries who have forsaken all to go out and offer that gift to the heathen, have often failed to believe the promise the Saviour gave to them, that of the hundredfold now in this life for everything they gave up?

The man who has believed and claimed it, enjoys the benefit of it *now,* just as the sinner who has claimed the gift of Eternal Life, reaps the benefit, and has the joy of it, from the moment he receives it.

FAITH AMONG LIONS

The Founders of the College forsook all to become missionaries in Africa. They broke up their home, left their only son, and their country and went to live among the heathen. For one period of eighteen months they never saw a white man; and during that time they lived in a two-roomed house of unburnt brick, with a mud floor. At another time, they were without a home for nearly two years, while they covered eleven thousand miles, travelling from one mission station to another. For about two months of every winter, they lived in a tent, travelling through the wilds of Portuguese East Africa, where they could not even take their dog, because of the tsetse-fly, which gives the sleeping sickness. They would travel about six hundred miles on foot, sleeping by night in the same forest as the lions, and other wild beasts. The only sound to break the silence of the night was the roar of a wild beast; and very often, when awakened by the king of the forest [the lions], they used to repeat to one another heartening verses from that wonderful ninety-first Psalm: "Thou shalt not be afraid of the terror by night.... There shall no evil befall thee...for He shall give His angels charge over thee.... Thou shalt tread upon the lion and the adder because he hath set his love upon me, therefore will I deliver him" (Psalm 91:5-14).

The joy of believing and proving these promises often made them break forth into singing; as Paul and Silas did in the prison at Philippi, when the angels came down to join them, and shook the prison and burst the doors open. (Was it to make room for so many celestial visitors?).

Many a time they sang:

> In God I have found a retreat
> Where I can securely abide;
> No refuge nor rest so complete,
> And here I intend to reside.
>
> The pestilence walking about
> When darkness has settled abroad,
> Can never compel me to doubt
> The presence and power of God.[2]

In the greatest danger, they never once doubted His Word or His Promise, but were always able to say: "Where He leads me I will follow."[3]

ONE LARGE FAMILY

Called back from Africa to found a new work in this country, can they not now say that God has given them, too, "the hundredfold?" The recent National Registration affords striking answer. To go out to the Mission Field, the Founders had left their one and only son behind.[4] But when recently the College family was registered the number then in residence was two hundred and fifteen; and there were other students who had not returned from their holidays. What an increase – from one absent child to a family circle which may soon be one thousand!

The youngest child on the register, Baby Herbert, only fifteen months old, had come from Vienna in his little basket about two months before.[5] He is only one of the hundreds of thousands of the Seed of Abraham who have had to flee from Hitler and Germany. From his birth he had to be fed from a soup kitchen, his father having been thrust into one of those concentration camps, ill-famed for so many abominable excesses, his only crime being that he was of Abraham's seed. But the promise still holds: "I will curse him that curseth thee" (Genesis 12:3). So Hitler and his Nazi régime cannot escape this time, for God has predicted their downfall. Surely for them it will be better that they had never been born.

To the missionaries who founded the College God has added "the hundredfold" in property as well as in children. He has given three estates, with mansions, other large buildings and nearly fifty acres of freehold land, to provide a home for their large mixed family. And this does not include the estate of the late Sir John Llewelyn, which the College has recently *bought, and which is nearly eight times as large as the other three estates put together. [*Penllergaer Estate].

Evidently God means that our family is soon to increase to eight times its present size! Already we have in residence a huge staff of ninety-five, which includes over twenty "degree" people on the educational side, and five qualified doctors. Among the sixty children already in residence are many Jewish refugees and children of missionaries.

The money spent last year on our family was £24,101 13s. 4d. [£1,625,400 in 2020] as shown in the Cash Statement; and this family, although so large, has only one Father, their Heavenly Father, to provide and care for them. And yet they have neither fear nor trepidation for the future. What a laughable thing it would be, if every family – following the lead of modern organisations – had to get a committee or a council, to handle their affairs, and then appeal to the outside world for money to provide food for them! Such a family would resemble Russia or Germany, where every bleak and half-starved home is organised by the State. But the Bible College community is like the large families of old Puritan England, where all looked to their father to provide for their daily needs, and their father looked direct to God. And God then, as now, "never faileth" (1 Kings 17:13-16).

THE CRUSE THAT NEVER FAILS

Although there was already a large family in the College to provide for, God revealed that we would not be any poorer, if we added a Home of Rest for Missionaries and also a Hospital in which to nurse them. At Sketty Isaf, God has already provided the Home of Rest, and missionaries staying there are only expected to contribute half the actual cost of their maintenance – *one guinea weekly [*£1 1s or £78 in 2020]. A few thousands of pounds have been spent already for the addition of ten bedrooms, a dining-room, a kitchen and a large garage. [This was an extension on Sketty Isaf House]. Here again the Lord has provided an excellent staff. The matron, [Miss Gwen Roderick] who is a trained nurse, joined the College years ago to use her skill for this purpose; and the other members of the staff, who have received the College blessing, have also dedicated their lives to minister to the missionaries.[6]

Here then, there are no quarrels; only loving service. Here we know in practice the wisdom of the exhortation to esteem others better than ourselves, and that it is indeed a privilege to serve those who have spent their lives in serving the Lord. The Master said: "Whosoever will be great among you, let him be your minister; and whosoever will be chief among you, let him be your servant" (Matthew 20:26-27).

When the prediction of a Home of Rest for Missionaries at Sketty Isaf was fulfilled, we were again able to raise our Ebenezer and say once more that "Hitherto hath the Lord helped us" (1 Samuel 7:12). May He help us to continue to be worthy ministers to those who minister Salvation.

HOSPITAL FOR MISSIONARIES

On the same principle, and because of His promise of the "Hundredfold," God had also to provide for those who had lost their health by working in unhealthy districts in tropical countries. Missionaries often need medical attention and careful nursing for months, after returning to the homeland; but many of them have no home of rest, nor the means to pay for proper medical treatment. This Hospital is for them, and for expectant mothers who, instead of going to maternity Hospitals, and paying about four guineas a week [£4 4s or £312 in 2020] for some weeks, can have free medical attention in God's Hospital, by only paying a guinea a week [£1 1s or £78 in 2020] for their board.[7]

To staff the Hospital God has had to call out the best doctors and nurses. The senior resident doctor gained honours in his final M.B. (Lond.), and he had held several hospital appointments before he was called to the College. But, realising the needs of those missionaries who were coming back from the Foreign Field, he went up to London for a further six months course in Tropical Medicine, and gained a diploma in that subject.

A young surgeon who was on the staff of the Cardiff Royal Infirmary, when called to the College, decided to take his F.R.C.S. so as to be better qualified for surgical practice in the College Hospital. Two other young doctors – a man and his wife – who had been practising for some time, were about to take up a large and lucrative practice in an industrial district. While on a visit to the College, they received the College blessing of forsaking all to follow the Lord Jesus, and were called to the staff of the Hospital. They broke up their lovely home, to become medical servants to the missionaries.[8]

One other, our first lady doctor, who came; five years ago, is Medical Officer for the women students. The present Hospital was intended to accommodate thirty-five patients, but owing to lack of room in the College and School, part of it has been used for class-rooms and sleeping accommodation.

The large Hospital, for two hundred patients, is to be built on the new estate, Penllergaer. There, the doctors, who are already lecturing in elementary medicine and surgery to the missionary students, will train the nurses for the State examinations, and the present nursing staff will also move to the new Hospital.[9]

Already we see the signs of greater days and greater service and greater blessings to come. But as yet we are only in the Preface of our Book of Faith and Service. The Book itself is yet to come. What a marvellous Book that Book of God's Full Dealings with the Bible College, is destined to be. Surely it will be the Book of the Future!

The Hospital built on the Derwen Fawr Estate 1939. The bungalow on the left was originally used as the Kindergarten (a pre-school)

CHAPTER 13

The Sum of it All

The Founders of the Bible College dedicated their lives to be an object lesson to all, of what may be accomplished by prayer and faith alone; their aim was to teach men and women that it is safe to trust God's Word and His promises. When the Lord called the Twelve and the Seventy, and sent them out in a small country like Israel, He charged them, saying: "Carry neither purse, nor scrip [knapsack]...for the labourer is worthy of his hire" (Luke 10:1-7), and on their return He asked: "When I sent you without purse, and scrip...lacked ye anything?" and they said: "Nothing" (Luke 22:35).

This ideal of faith and complete trust in the living God, has not been generally followed since the days of the Early Church, though in every generation a few outstanding men, like George Müller, have lived up to it. Thirty years ago, the Founders were called to "forsake all" (Luke 14:33), "to sell all that ye have" (Luke 18:22), and to trust God for temporal as well as for spiritual needs. So, after proving God day by day for the first few years of their married life [from December 1910 onwards], it became as easy to live upon God's Promises, as previously it was to live on a salary or on money in the bank.

Many a time the Founders had to walk to the Railway Station without money for their tickets, and once or twice they had to enter the queue at the booking-office, without money or tickets. Yet both were forthcoming before the train departed. Who can forget hearing the story of how the Director had to stand in the queue at the booking-office for tickets to London when he and his wife were on their way to Africa, and how he only received his fee [his deliverance] when he was next but one to the top of the queue, where he would ask for his tickets. With what a shout of victory he came away, saying: "The God of Moses who opened the Red Sea can never, never fail!"

Hundreds of similar instances could be related of how God has answered believing prayer; the very amount needed arriving at the right moment; so there was no loophole for the Devil to say that it came by chance. Now, after thirty years, we are as much at home in asking God for a thousand pounds, as in those days we were in asking Him to meet an essential need of ten pounds.

RECENT ANSWERS

Here are some instances of answers to prayer in the last two or three weeks, while these chapters were being written. For weeks past every Monday has been a Day of Prayer; and two weeks ago there was a need of £100 [£6,550 in 2020] on the Monday. That day a letter came from Chicago, [in America], with no name given, but enclosing a draft for £100 to be paid to us through the Westminster Bank. The next Day of Prayer came with a need of about £50 and that very day a cheque for £50 [£3,275 in 2020] was received, and last Saturday (November 8th, 1939) £1,000 came to hand! [£65,500 in 2020] And this week another £1,000 has been released for the new estate, Penllergaer.

WHY DON'T WE TRUST?

This life of trusting God for temporal needs has been lost in the Church. Christians pray daily: "Give us this day our daily bread" (Matthew 6:11), and yet are unable to trust God to give it day by day. If young people, who have been called to forsake all, and become the Lord's disciples, have a claim on Him to supply their daily needs, what sense is there in their throwing up their salary, and going round the country on deputation work for the sake of getting their need, or their Mission's needs, supplied? The Promise is: "Seek ye first the Kingdom of God; *and all these things shall be added unto you*" (Matthew 6:33).

The Lord built the Bible College of Wales, so that young men and women, who have had the "Call" to be ambassadors for Him in foreign lands, should look to Him alone to supply their personal needs. What a disgrace it would be if our Ambassador in Washington, going round America, should appeal to people to supply his needs, because he was not able to trust the King of England. How much more then should we trust the King of kings, who is the Owner of "the silver and the gold?" (Haggai 2:8).

Young men and women, who have had three years training in the College, have been able to trust God for their board and residence (which is given to them at less than half the actual cost), and then to trust Him still when they reach the land of their adoption. The Word of God says: "Be careful for nothing, but in everything by prayer and supplication, with thanksgiving, let your requests be made known unto God.... My God shall supply all your needs" (Philippians 4:6, 19).

FAITH COLLEGES EVERYWHERE

There are many who have been trained in the College – the School of Faith – working in nearly all foreign lands where there are Missions. There will be room on the new estate, Penllergaer, to train hundreds, who will, after training, go out, "taking nothing from the Gentiles" (3 John 1:7).

The Lord is going to prepare hundreds of young people, who, after spending three or four years in the Bible College of Wales, will go out and found Colleges in every country to reach Every Creature; men and women, who will not only be able to teach Greek, Hebrew, Church History, Nursing, etc., but teach the students to trust God to supply their personal needs. Then, instead of only a few missionaries and native workers, working on lonely stations, there will be thousands (including natives), trained in the Colleges, available for missionary work. These too, will by learning in the School of Faith, will find that living faith becomes substance. They will be like Pastor Hsi in China, who was able to trust God to supply his personal needs and to inspire many Christian Chinese to do the same, just as men like Müller, Chapman and others inspired their friends and followers.

The College has already bought a freehold property in Paris[1] where there is a large Mission Hall and room for students in residence. There we have opened a College, which is staffed by those who have spent three or four years in the Swansea College. We are convinced that the Holy Spirit will bring the College Vision (the Gospel to Every Creature) to fruition, God will train His own missionaries in the Colleges and will send them out by the hundreds. There will be no conflict with those Christians who are not able to live the full *life of faith,* and therefore have not seen the Vision as 'we have seen it.'

Our Secondary Schools, for all missionaries' children, will enable these little ones to join the College, and learn the life of faith and become teachers and nurses in the Colleges in foreign lands. And so follow worthily in the footsteps of their parents. Our Home of Rest for Missionaries; and the Hospital, will be enlarged as the years go on. No one will be asked to pay more than half the actual cost of maintenance (God supplying the other half through us by gifts which last year, were nearly four times as much as all the fees received put together).

Every summer there is held on the College estates, the "Every Creature" Conference, and scores of persons have been blessed in these Conferences and many thousands are destined to be blessed in future.

So then these predictions are an outcome of a walk with God for over thirty years, of treading a path of complete reliance on Him for temporal as well as spiritual needs, during which time: "We have lacked nothing" (Luke 22:35), having taken out of God's Treasury thousands and thousands of pounds in gifts without a single appeal to man. We can say: "We love our Master, and we will not go out free" (Exodus 21:5-6).

PEACE AT EVENTIDE[2]

One last word to everybody. Be of good cheer. After the prediction of God's settlement with Hitler and the Nazi régime is fulfilled, the countries for some years will not be troubled with further menaces, similar to that of Hitlerism. It will then be, as in King David's time, after God gave him peace on every hand, when he established the nation, and prepared to build a House for the Lord, and gathered for it over a thousand million pounds, when silver became in Jerusalem like stones.

The Lord has promised to "open His treasury to the College," and that they are to "lend to nations." And the first nation to receive is to be the Jews. He has promised to give to the College a gift of £100,000 to buy land and houses in the Holy Land[3] (see Jeremiah 32:43-44), and to send back the Jewish children after four years in our Secondary Schools, and three years in one of our Colleges. They will be among the host of evangelists, who will prepare the way for the return of the Lord. Who will be able to withstand their fervent presentation of the Good News of the God of their Fathers? Who will not wish to serve their new-found King, our Lord Jesus Christ? Their Saviour and ours.

The sands of time are sinking,
  The dawn of Heaven breaks
The summer morn I've sighed for,
  The fair sweet morn awakes:

Dark, dark hath been the midnight,
  But dayspring is at hand,
And glory, glory dwelleth
  In Immanuel's land.[4]

The Bible College of Wales

CASH STATEMENT

for the year ended 31st March 1939.

Dr.   **Cr.**

Receipts.

Year to 31st March 1938 £	Receipts.	£	s	d
—	To Balance at Bank 1/4/38	2	3	4
5,435 4 5	" Receipts from College, Day School, Boarding School, Missionary Home, Hospital & Conference Fees	5,327	17	9
		5,330	1	1
600	" Capital receipts	—	—	—
6,080	" Gifts received	18,771	12	3
£12,115		£24,101	13	4

Payments.

Year to 31st March 1938 £	Payments.	£	s	d
7,849	By Expenses in connection with the College, School, Missionary Home & Hospital, including Rates, Taxes, Fuel & Lighting, Repairs, Salaries & Wages, Provisions & Miscellaneous Expenses	12,270	13	0
3,831	" Purchase of land, New buildings, Additions & Equipment of a Capital nature, & Bank Balances	10,804	10	4
£11,680		£23,075	3	4
435	" Gifts to Missionaries & others	982	13	6
—	" Balance at Bank 31/3/39	43	16	6
£12,115		£24,101	13	4

I certify the above CASH STATEMENT to be in accordance with the books and vouchers of the Bible College and Missionary School.

Derwen Fawr,
Swansea.
11th April 1939.

H. S. W. Seward.
Chartered Accountant.

The Bible College of Wales Cash Statement for the year ended 31 March 1939. Notice the value of the Receipts and Payments were exactly the same income of £24,101 or approximately £1,625,400 in 2020! There was no surplus money held in the bank to draw from, but trust in God who said He would supply all your *need* (Philippians 4:19), not wants or desires. God pays His own invoices, what He has sanctioned. God's work, done God's way in His timing, will not lack His resources. God pays His own bills.

GOD
CHALLENGES
THE
DICTATORS

—

DOOM OF NAZIS PREDICTED

REES HOWELLS

A 1939 hardback of *God Challenges the Dictators* which has
been converted into greyscale. The original colour
was red with black lettering and framing.

END OF BOOK – *God Challenges The Dictators*

EPILOGUE

Jesus said to His disciples, "The harvest truly is plentiful, but the labourers are few. Therefore pray the Lord of the harvest to send out labourers into His harvest" (Matthew 9:38).

The Vision of 26th December 1934 given to Rees Howells in Derwen Fawr House, Sketty, Swansea, became known as the Every Creature Vision / Commission. It was believed that the Gospel should be given to all mankind, to every tribe, nation and tongue within thirty years – a generation. They were to take personal responsibility to intercede for the Gospel to go to Every Creature and to live sacrificial lives in order to train and prepare people for the mission field.

Rees Howells was not the first person to believe that the consummation of the age would be in "this generation" (thirty years), as others Christian workers had mentioned it from the 1860s onwards. Men such as Hudson Taylor, founder of the China Inland Mission, A. B. Simpson, founder of the Christian and Missionary Alliance and John R. Mott, missionary statesman, all preached the possibility of evangelising the world in their generation. In 1910, the first International Missionary Conference was held in Edinburgh, Scotland, its motto was: 'The Evangelisation of the World in this Generation.'

By June 1936, at the Bible College of Wales (BCW) there were one hundred and seventy staff and students praying and interceding three hours a day for the Every Creature Commission to see its fulfilment.

First, once every tribe, nation and tongue has heard the Good News then Jesus can return – the Second Coming. People need an opportunity to hear the Good News to repent, to forsake their sin and to put their trust in the finished work of Jesus Christ. He died and rose again so that we can have eternal life in Him. It is God's grace and mercy, His free gift to mankind that Jesus willingly took the sins of the world upon Himself when He was beaten and crucified, died, buried and rose again after three days; so that we can go free and have a relationship with God through His Son Jesus Christ who shed His blood for mankind on the cross of Calvary. The apostle Paul wrote: 'That if you confess with your mouth the Lord Jesus and believe in your heart that

God has raised Him from the dead, you will be saved. For with the heart one believes unto righteousness, and with the mouth confession is made unto salvation. ...For "Whoever calls on the name of the Lord shall be saved." How then shall they call on Him in whom they have not believed? And how shall they believe in Him of whom they have not heard? And how shall they hear without a preacher? And how shall they preach unless they are sent?' (Romans 10:9-14).

Jesus declared, "And this Gospel of the Kingdom will be preached in all the world as a witness to all the nations, and then the end will come" (Matthew 24:14). Jesus stated, "And the Gospel must first be preached to all the nations" (Mark 13:10).

Peter wrote: 'Looking for and *hastening* the coming of the day of God, because of which the heavens will be dissolved, being on fire...' (2 Peter 3:12). It was revealed in Heaven: 'And they sang a new song, saying, "You [Jesus] are worthy to take the scroll, and to open its seals; for You were slain, and have redeemed us to God by Your blood out of every tribe and tongue and people and nation" (Revelation 5:9).

Second, Rees Howells believed that 10,000 people would be raised up like himself, *full* of the Holy Spirit to go into all the world and preach the Gospel in the power of the Spirit.

Third, Rees Howells believed that God would finance these men and women and as a *sign*, a gift of £10,000 would be given to the Bible College of Wales which was received in July 1938, worth £674,400 in 2020.

The Vision Rees Howells received added great emphasis on individuals, for their responsibility in world evangelisation which meant a full surrender and consecration. The apostle Paul wrote: 'I beseech you therefore, brethren, by the mercies of God, that you present your bodies a living sacrifice, holy, acceptable to God, which is your reasonable service' (Romans 12:1). This has to be coupled with an enduement of power for service. Jesus said, "But you shall receive power when the Holy Spirit has come upon you; and you shall be witnesses to Me in Jerusalem, and in all Judea and Samaria, and to the end of the earth" (Acts 1:8). Jesus said, "Go into all the world and preach the Gospel to Every Creature" (Mark 16:15), which became the motto of BCW and the Vision was presented to the staff and students of BCW on 1st January 1935. A contemporary interpretation of the Vision can be summed up as: Go ye (Mark 16:15), give ye (Luke 9:13), pray ye (Matthew 9:38) and ideally do all three, in the power of the Spirit (Acts 1:8), for the glory of God and the exultation of Jesus Christ.

Serve Him, obey Him and abide in Him (John 15:1-11). Go and make disciples of all nations (Matthew 28:19).

It was during the war years that Rees Howells and his team of around 120 intercessors played major roles in national and international intercessions for world events. Rees and his team's first international intercession was seen in March 1936 when the Locarno Treaty was broken – Germany went into the demilitarised zone – the Rhineland, but a European War was averted. But their international intercession began after Easter 1936 when the Holy Spirit descended on BCW and each individual put his or her life on the line and fully and unequivocally surrendered all. The summer of 1938 (September) saw their intercessions over the Munich Crisis when Hitler invaded Czechoslovakia and once again, war was averted.

Rees Howells had believed and predicted in January 1940 that World War II would end by Whit-Sunday (Pentecost) 1941. This was not in *God Challenges the Dictators,* because of its earlier publication date of mid-December 1939. Like all of Rees Howells' major predictions; he announced them to the media as a sign and a testament and they were always printed in the local papers and sometimes the national ones. World War II did not end until 1945 with an estimated total loss of 55 million lives. In the eyes of many, Rees Howells and BCW was deemed a failure and he was labelled a 'false prophet' by some. Some said that the predictions were false, others, that it was another death – the grain which had to die before it could bear fruit; but God had bigger purposes involved. It was at this point that BCW lost a lot of its support from those who merely came to the public meetings for the wrong reasons. It was a season of sifting, shaking and pruning (John 15), and only the truly committed stood loyal and it was these genuine warriors – the 300 of Gideon's men (Judges 7) who did the real battle through the hard and trying years that lay ahead.

Final Years and Passing the Baton

Rees Howells' intercessions during World War II, alongside his dedicated team at the Bible College of Wales, witnessed world events changing by prevailing prayer and the free world was liberated from the tyranny of the World War II dictators. Christian England never gave in and Rees Howells and the staff of BCW never lost faith, but believed and pressed forward in victory! Rees Howells suffered several heart attacks in the previous months before he died in 1950. For the four preceding days before he passed on, he was in and out of consciousness. His last words were, "Victory...Hallelujah" – uttered on 12th February 1950 and he passed into glory the following day at 10am on Monday, 13th February. Within one hour, his son, thirty-eight year old Samuel Rees Howells called the entire staff of the Bible College of Wales and School together and they rededicated their lives to God to carry on with the Vision, to reach Every Creature for Christ.

In the 1960s, Samuel Rees Howells gave the College a renewed sense of vision and leadership, as he prepared them to continue to be responsible for the Vision of world evangelisation, not in a limited time, but for the rest of their lives. The intercession was now a lifetime commitment to pray, give and go until all are reached. Samuel also always remained committed to the distribution of the Scriptures and large sums of money were used in printing and distributing Bibles, as well as supporting missionaries in the field across the globe. These were not only former BCW students, but hundreds of other ministries, working and labouring in the harvest fields of the world in a variety of capacities.

Thank you for taking the time to read this book. Please write a short review on your favourite review site and give a shout out on social media. Thank you.

Social Media
Facebook: /ByFaithMedia
Twitter: @ByFaithMedia
Youtube: /ByFaithMedia
Pinterest: /ByFaithMedia
Instagram: @ByFaithMedia

Rees Howells (1879-1950)
www.facebook.com/ReesHowellsIntercessor

Samuel Rees Howells (1912-2004)
www.facebook.com/SamuelReesHowells

Rees Howells and Samuel Rees Howells Related Books
Directors of the Bible College of Wales
(Hardbacks and paperbacks)

Samuel Rees Howells A Life of Intercession: The Legacy of Prayer and Spiritual Warfare of an Intercessor by Richard Maton, Paul Backholer and Mathew Backholer. An in-depth look at the intercessions of Samuel Rees Howells alongside the faith principles that he learnt from his father, Rees Howells, and under the leading and guidance of the Holy Spirit.

Samuel, Son and Successor of Rees Howells: Director of the Bible College of Wales – A Biography by Richard Maton edited by Mathew Backholer. The life of Samuel and his ministry at the College and the support he received from numerous staff and students as the history of the Bible College of Wales unfolds.

Rees Howells' God Challenges the Dictators, Doom of Axis Powers Predicted: Victory for Christian England and Release of Europe Through Intercession and Spiritual Warfare, Bible College of Wales by Mathew Backholer. This is the story behind the story of *God Challenges the Dictators* (GCD), Rees Howells' only published book, before, during and after publication which is centred around World War II. Read how extracts of GCD were aired over occupied parts of Europe, and how Hitler and leading Nazi officials were sent copies in 1940!

God Challenges the Dictators, Doom of the Nazis Predicted: The Destruction of the Third Reich Foretold by the Director of Swansea Bible College, An Intercessor from Wales by Rees Howells and Mathew Backholer. Available for the first time in 80 years – fully annotated. Discover how Rees Howells built a large ministry by faith in times of economic chaos and learn from the predictions he made during times of national crisis.

Continued over the page

Rees Howells, Vision Hymns of Spiritual Warfare & Intercessory Declarations: World War II Songs of Victory, Intercession, Praise and Worship, Israel and the Every Creature Commission by Mathew Backholer. A collection of rare hymns and choruses from the Bible College of Wales (BCW) under Rees Howells' Directorship composed by different people. Drawn from three different BCW hymn books spanning the pivotal years of 1939-1948 and brought to life for the first time in more than seventy years. Many of the hymns reveal the theology, spiritual battles, and history during the dark days of World War II and the years surrounding it. From Emperor Haile Selassie of Ethiopia, Hitler's predicted downfall, to the Nation of Israel being born in a day and the glories beyond. How Jesus Christ is still on the Throne, victory was assured, the Nazis' would be defeated and the Every Creature Commission would see its fulfilment. Other moving and stirring hymns and chorus are evangelistic in nature used within the College Chapel when all were welcomed. Some reveal Jesus' sacrifice, the Vision finances, the Second Coming, and the glory and splendour of the New Jerusalem in Heaven's eternal glory. More than a collection of rare hymns and chorus, but a revelation, explanation and historical analysis behind many hymns, coupled with historical events and the authentic voice of Rees Howells. Including letters, rare and never-seen-before photos, fully digitally enhanced plus three never-before published poems about Mr and Mrs Howells, and the BCW staff member arrested in Paris under the Nazis, his Divine escape and return to BCW in 1942.

The Holy Spirit in a Man: Spiritual Warfare, Intercession, Faith, Healings and Miracles by R. B. Watchman edited by Paul Backholer and Mathew Backholer. One man's compelling journey of faith and intercession, a remarkable modern day story of miracles and faith to inspire and encourage. (One chapter relates to the Bible College of Wales and Watchman's visit).

Holy Spirit Power: Knowing the Voice, Guidance and Person of the Holy Spirit: Inspiration from Rees Howells, Evan Roberts, D. L. Moody, Duncan Campbell and Other Channels of God's Divine Fire by Paul Backholer.

Books by Mathew Backholer

The majority of the following books are available as paperbacks and eBooks on a number of different platforms worldwide. Some are also available as hardbacks.

Historical
- Hardback collector's edition (and paperback): God Challenges the Dictators, Doom of the Nazis Predicted: The Destruction of the Third Reich Foretold by the Director of Swansea Bible College an Intercessor from Wales (Rees Howells and Mathew Backholer).
- Hardback Collector's edition: Rees Howells' God Challenges the Dictators, Doom of Axis Powers Predicted: Victory for Christian England and Release of Europe Through Intercession. (This is the story behind the story of *God Challenges the Dictators,* before, during and after publication which is centred around World War II. The book includes letters to Prime Minister Winston Churchill, Press Releases from Rees Howells, plus newspaper articles and adverts, and what Rees Howells said and wrote about his only published work).
- Hardback Collector's edition: Rees Howells, Vision Hymns of Spiritual Warfare & Intercessory Declarations: World War II Songs of Victory, Intercession, Praise and Worship, Israel and the Every Creature Commission.

Christian Revivals and Awakenings
- Revival Fires and Awakenings, Thirty-Six Visitations of the Holy Spirit. (Also available as a hardback).
- Understanding Revival and Addressing the Issues it Provokes.
- Global Revival, Worldwide Outpourings, Forty-Three Visitations of the Holy Spirit.
- Revival Answers, True and False Revivals.
- Revival Fire, 150 Years of Revivals.
- Reformation to Revival, 500 Years of God's Glory.

Continued over the page

Christian Discipleship and Spiritual Growth
- Christianity Rediscovered, In Pursuit of God and the Path to Eternal Life. Book 1.
- Christianity Explored. Book 2.
- Extreme Faith, On Fire Christianity.
- Discipleship For Everyday Living, Christian Growth.

Christian Missions (Travel with a Purpose)
- Short-Term Missions, A Christian Guide to STMs.
- How to Plan, Prepare and Successfully Complete Your Short-Term Mission.

World Travel
- Budget Travel, A Guide to Travelling on a Shoestring, Explore the World.
- Travel the World and Explore for Less than $50 a Day, the Essential Guide.

Sources and Notes

Foreword

1. See *Rees Howells' God Challenges the Dictators, Doom of Axis Powers Predicted: Victory for Christian England and Release of Europe Through Intercession and Spiritual Warfare, Bible College of Wales* by Mathew Backholer, ByFaith Media 2020, page 152. This book is the complete story behind *God Challenges the Dictators* by Rees Howells and includes many never before published photos, and historical facts which have never before been published or have lay undiscovered for eighty years. It is the story behind the story, before, during and after publication centred around World War II and includes many historical letters, newspaper articles and press releases.

2. *Rees Howells' God Challenges the Dictators, Doom of Axis Powers Predicted: Victory for Christian England and Release of Europe Through Intercession and Spiritual Warfare, Bible College of Wales* by Mathew Backholer, ByFaith Media 2020, pages 17-18 and 50.

3. Ibid. page 40.

4. Ibid. page 70.

5. Ibid. pages 24 and 165.

Preface

1. *See Tortured For Christ* by Richard Wurmbrand, Release International, 1967, 2012.

2. *Rees Howells Intercessor* by Norman Grubb, Lutterworth Press, 1952, pages 214-216 and 239.

3. Ibid., pages 217-218.

4. *Rees Howells' God Challenges the Dictators, Doom of Axis Powers Predicted: Victory for Christian England and Release of Europe Through Intercession and Spiritual Warfare, Bible College of Wales* by Mathew Backholer, ByFaith Media 2020. It is the story behind the story, before, during and after publication centred around World War II.

5. See *Samuel Rees Howells: A Life of Intercession* by Richard Maton, ByFaith Media, 2012, 2017, pages 80-83.

6. See *Rees Howells Intercessor* by Norman Grubb, Lutterworth Press, 1952, chapter 34.

7. Ibid., page 243.

8. https://www.bankofengland.co.uk/monetary-policy/inflation/inflation-calculator.

Introduction

1. One copy of *God Challenges the Dictators* was owned by a staff member of the Bible College of Wales (BCW) who was present during the war years who passed away more than sixty years later at BCW. Her book revealed that she had pasted in extracts of newspapers columns from World War II and written annotations in the margins aligning what Rees Howells had predicted with what had happened.

2. History records that Adolf Hitler killed himself in a bunker in Berlin, Germany, when he knew that the Nazi régime had been defeated and the allies were closing in.

3. See Epilogue, the Vision was given in December 1934 and the book was published in December 1939, hence five years had elapsed and there were

twenty-five years remaining. In 1999, Wycliffe Bible Translators developed and adopted a project 'Vision 2025' which commenced the following year, where over the next 25 years they planned to translate or to begin to translate the Bible into every language that needed it. It is a *great* vision to have and they have been working hard towards it for the past twenty years and more than 2,100 translations (Sept 2019) still need to begin.

4. The phrase 'when peace will be upon the earth, and goodwill towards men' is an allusion to the "Christmas" verse in the Bible of Luke 2:14 when the angel of the Lord announced to the shepherds in the fields at night, "For there is born to you this day in the city of David a Saviour, who is Christ the Lord. And this will be the sign to you: You will find a Babe wrapped in swaddling cloths, lying in a manger." And suddenly there was with the angel a multitude of the heavenly host praising God and saying, "Glory to God in the highest, and on earth peace, goodwill toward men!" (Luke 2:11-14).

5. This hymn is the fourth stanza of five of *Who Is On The Lord's Side*, written by Frances Ridley Havergal (1836-1879). She lived in the Caswell district and when Rees and Lizzie Howells were on 'holiday' in the Swansea and Mumbles area they visited the house where she lived and died, on Caswell Avenue, Caswell, Swansea.

Chapter 1

1. Czar can also be spelt Tzar and Tsar.

2. See *Revival Fires and Awakenings, Thirty-Six Visitations of the Holy Spirit: A Call to Holiness, Prayer and Intercession for the Nations* by Mathew Backholer, ByFaith Media, 2009, 2017, chapter 3. And *Great Christian Revivals* DVD, ByFaith Media, 2016 which documents the Evangelical Revival (1739-1791), as well as other revivals in the United Kingdom.

3. See *Reformation to Revival, 500 Years of God's Glory: Sixty Revivals, Awakenings and Heaven-Sent Visitations of the Holy Spirit* by Mathew Backholer, ByFaith Media, 2018, chapter 9.

4. Ludwig Müller was a German Theologian who was associated with the Nazis in the 1920s and was appointed Reich Bishop by Adolf Hitler in 1933. As an anti-Christ and anti-Jewish theologian he caused much trouble for Evangelical Christians in Germany and permitted the Gestapo to monitor the churches and youth groups under his care. At the end of the war he took his own life.

5. Martin Niemöller was an outspoken Lutheran pastor who initially embraced Hitler and his policies because unemployment was decreasing and German prestige was rising. However, in the 1930s he denounced Nazism and was arrested in 1937, and held in two concentration camps from 1938 to 1945. He was widely known for his poem from 1946 in the German language of which there are several variations in English:

> First they came for the socialists, and I did not speak out –
>   Because I was not a socialist.
> Then they came for the trade unionists, and I did not speak out –
>   Because I was not a trade unionist.
> Then they came for the Jews, and I did not speak out –
>   Because I was not a Jew.
> Then they came for me – and there was no one left to speak for me.

Chapter 2

1. For more about Martin Luther and the Reformation which began in 1517 in Germany, and spread to other countries across Europe, see *Reformation to Revival, 500 Years of God's Glory: Sixty Revivals, Awakenings and Heaven-*

Sent Visitations of the Holy Spirit by Mathew Backholer, ByFaith Media, 2018, chapters 3-5.

2. The 'thirty years' was not part of the original revelation concerning 'no European war' but because Rees Howells believed the Vision would be completed in thirty years, he came to this *assumption* which was proved incorrect. "For My thoughts are not your thoughts, nor are your ways My ways," says the Lord (Isaiah 55:8).

Chapter 4

1. Rees Howells received more than one hundred letters (from 1937-1940) often accompanied with photos from parents (Jews and non-Jews) and older siblings across Europe, begging and pleading him to accept their children or younger siblings, yet his hands were tied. Many applicants wanted places for their child or children at the Boarding School, others pleaded for asylum and would take on any duties or roles so as to escape the horrors of Europe. It took months for the Home Office to grant decisions. The author has read some of these heart-wrenching letters (and some of the replies), especially as the fate of most of those concerned was sealed in the concentration camps of Europe. In May 1939, Rees Howells was prepared to sell the three sites of Glynderwen, Derwen Fawr and Sketty Isaf which had been valued at nearly £100,000 and use this amount to look after a minimum of 1,000 Jewish refugee children, though they calculated they could take 2,000 children. One thousand children would cost £50,000 (£3,274,600 in 2020) per year. Even the local newspapers reported on this 'Welsh George Müller.' Rees would be liable for the children's board, keep and education until their eighteenth birthday. Due to British Government restrictions on immigration, Rees Howells was unable to take in the large number of Jewish refugees that he wanted to save from the Nazi régime.

2. See point 3. under Introduction in Sources and Notes.

3. The first two lines of this hymn are the same as *Blessed and Glorious King* by Thomas Hodgson Mundell (1849-1934). However this hymn is probably one composed by Ardis Butterfield, a staff member of the Bible College of Wales. She was an anointed singer and songwriter, whose ministry in the Spirit would lift the worship during the dark days of World War II.

Chapter 5

1. On 15th June 1944, at the 9:45pm service (one of three services a day held at the College during the war years), Rees Howells acknowledged that 'to save the German nation the Director [Rees Howells] would be willing for God not to make the Divine Intervention. In such an open way, as at first he expected it to be.' The following day at the 7pm service, it was stated, 'the Director is feeling for the people of Germany as he did four years ago for the people of our country [during the blitzes]. An intercession will have to be made for the German nation as Moses made an atonement for the children of Israel. What is the price that will have to be paid?' At the 9:45pm meeting on the same day, the questioned was asked, 'What intercession does God call for, for Germany to be set free? She is entering into her death now. [The Second Front had begun and 2,000 Allied planes were bombing Nazi occupied targets every night as well as civilian areas to break the Nazi morale]. Will He tell us what her resurrection is to be?'

2. The Moravians were originally from Bohemia, the native Czechs who had a Reformation in the late fourteenth century under various Bohemian preachers and in the early fifteenth century under John Hus. They were also influenced by

the writings of John Wycliff of England and had suffered persecution in Bohemia and Moravia for their Christian beliefs for two centuries until they decided to move. In 1747 and 1749, England passed Acts of Parliament recognising the Moravian fraternity as an ancient Protestant Episcopal Church, and granted it civil and religious privileges at home and in British colonies. There was a revival amongst the Moravian community at Herrnhut in 1727 and from that one small village community more than one hundred missionaries went out in twenty-five years. Dr. Warneck, a German historian of Protestant Missions wrote: 'This small church in twenty years called into being more missions than the whole Evangelical Church had done in two centuries.' By 1757, Moravian missionaries were ministering in nearly every country in Europe and they went into Asia, South Africa, Australia and North and South America. For more information about the Moravians, the revival of 1727 and their mission advance see *Global Revival, Worldwide Outpourings, Forty-Three Visitations of the Holy Spirit: The Great Commission* by Mathew Backholer, ByFaith Media, 2010, 2017, chapter 8.

John Wesley in his *Journal* for 1st January 1739 wrote: 'Mr Hall, Kinchin, Ingham, Whitefield, Hutchins, and my brother Charles, were present at our love-feast in Fetters Lane [in London, England, at a Moravian Society], with about sixty of our brethren. About three in the morning, as we were continuing instant in prayer, the power of God came mightily upon us, insomuch that many cried out for exceeding joy, and many fell to the ground. As soon as we were recovered a little from that awe and amazement, at the presence of His Majesty, we broke out with one voice, "We praise thee, O God, we acknowledge thee to be the Lord." ' Fetters Lane is now known as Fetter Lane in EC4 London. On this site was the above revival and a Moravian Congregation was founded there on 10th November 1742. It became the Moravian Headquarters in 1872 and was destroyed in an air-raid on 11th May 1941.

3. The phrase 'we must build Jerusalem in England's green and pleasant land' is an allusion to William Blake's poem *And Did Those Feet in Ancient Time* (c.1808), as part of his Preface to his epic *Milton: A Poem in Two Books*. It is better known as the hymn, *Jerusalem* with music (1916) by Sir Hubert Parry. The first and last stanzas are:

> And did those feet in ancient time,
> Walk upon England's mountains green:
> And was the holy Lamb of God,
> On England's pleasant pastures seen!
>
> I will not cease from mental fight,
> Nor shall my sword sleep in my hand:
> Till we have built Jerusalem,
> In England's green and pleasant Land.

Chapter 6

1. On 18th September 1947, Mr Grunhut of Vienna, Austria, stayed at the Bible College of Wales for a holiday, reported a local newspaper. Twice Mr Grunhut escaped the gas chamber in a Polish concentration camp – forty-two of his relatives died in the Holocaust including his own parents. His two children came to Britain as refugees and the Bible College of Wales raised them – Herbert (the baby in the basket) and his older brother, Ervin. Herbert "Bert" Grunhut was a regular visitor to the Bible College and its grounds and died in January 2019 in his eightieth year. The funeral service was held at Siloam Baptist Church, Killay, Swansea, less than three miles away from the Bible College of Wales.

2. Before the Lord Jesus Christ can return to earth, the Second Coming, Jesus said, "This Gospel of the Kingdom shall be preached in all the world for a witness unto all nations; and then shall the end come" (Matthew 24:14). For Rees Howells, if the Every Creature Commission could be completed in thirty years, a generation, or twenty-five years in 1939 as the clock was counting, then there could not be anything hindering the Lord's return, to begin His Millennial Reign on earth. It was Rees Howells' logical conclusion: If this happens (Every Creature) then this can happen (Second Coming). Peter wrote: 'Looking for and *hastening* the coming of the day of God...' (2 Peter 3:12). We can hasten or speed up the Second Coming by reaching the unevangelised of every tribe, tongue, people group and nation, who will stand before the throne of God (Revelation 5:9). Also see point 3 below.

3. When Rees Howells was writing in 1939, the Jews had not yet returned to the Holy Land (another condition for the Second Coming), the Land of Promise, the land of Israel as a nation, when the Nation of Israel was 'born in a day' (Isaiah 66:8) in May 1948. "Then the Lord thy God will turn thy captivity, and have compassion upon thee, and will return and gather thee from all the nations, whither the Lord thy God hath scattered thee" (Deuteronomy 30:3). *The Times* newspaper for 19th September 1938 notes: 'An application is to be made to the Home Secretary to permit the Bible College of Wales at Swansea to accept 40 young Jewish refugees aged between 18 and 20. It is proposed to teach them languages and send them to the Holy Land after three years.'

Three years training at the Bible College of Wales was standard. Rees Howells actively and firmly believed in 'hastening the coming day of God' (2 Peter 3:12) and assisting in the re-gathering of Jews back to the Holy Land. The 'sons of the promise' would be introduced to Jesus Christ the Messiah at the Bible College of Wales (age 18+) or the Bible School (ages 5-18) and it was hoped that they would go to the Holy Land to evangelise and 'prepare the way for the Lord,' as John the Baptist did, calling people to "repent" and look for the coming Messiah.

The newspaper headline from the *Western Mail,* 18th December 1939 read:
"Bible College Wants Refugees – Jews Instead of Spaniards"
'Application has been made to the Home Office by the Bible College of Wales, Swansea, for permission to take 20 Jewish refugees who have written from Germany, Austria, and Italy. Among them are four doctors. The College authorities have also asked Swansea Corporation [the Council] for tenancy of the mansion [at Penllergaer] used to house Spanish refugee children, so that it may be used for further Jewish refugees. The College hopes to be able to house 100 refugees. Rev. Rees Howells, College Director, states that a woman in the Holy Land who had read of the prediction from the Bible College that there would be no war, was so stirred that she wrote to him offering terms for taking over a hotel and sanatorium in the Holy Land, for a College and Hospital for Jewish refugees. Mr Howells says he will go to the Holy Land to negotiate for the property and also to try to purchase land for these refugees.'

It is important to stress that Rees Howells wanted Jewish refugees as opposed to Spanish ones because the Jews were most at risk from Hitler's wrath and genocide. There were Spanish refugees at the Bible College of Wales' Bible School, later known as Emmanuel Grammar School. In March 1937, Evangelist Parillo from Spain and his four children (Alejandro, Guillermo, Margarita and Elia) found a refuge at the Bible College of Wales. His wife and their baby were in France and later were reunited with their family in Swansea.

Chapter 7

1. Rees Howells' quote '*to build the largest Bible College* by prayer and faith alone,' (my emphasis) can be interpreted in several ways. In 1939, when *God Challenges the Dictators* was written Rees Howells owned 270 acres at Penllergaer, Swansea district, and 50 acres at the three sites of Glynderwen, Sketty Isaf and Derwen Fawr at Sketty, Swansea. This is a total of 320 acres, making it the largest Bible College in Britain, (which in addition was run by prayer and faith alone). Also, in 1929 there were 130+ students in residence, 140 students in residence in another year, 90 students in 1935 and in 1936 they had received more than 100 applicants. No other College in Britain had this many students thus making it the 'largest Bible College' in Britain based on the student body. In 1939 there were 95 members of staff, the largest number of staff at any Bible College in Britain, though this included staff for the School etc. whilst some staff members had duties in the College and the School. 20 out of the 95 staff had degrees (very important in academia) and were on the educational side. There were also five qualified doctors because the College had its own Hospital and taught tropical medicine and healthcare for the mission field. The Hospital was commandeered for a period of time during World War II to help with casualties of the war.

Rees Howells from the *Twelfth Session Annual Report* of 1936, wrote: 'While there is a dearth of students in most Colleges, the Bible College of Wales *cannot accommodate all the applicants* [my emphasis]. Last year [1935] there were 90 students in residence and over 30 of them joined the same Mission, the Worldwide Evangelization Crusade (WEC), and others went to Japan, China etc. *More than a hundred applicants for this new term have been accepted, and others are asked to wait until the New Year.*' (My emphasis).

In chapter 7 of *God Challenges the Dictators,* Rees Howells wrote: 'Thus *was founded* [my emphasis] the largest College of its kind in the country, with, at one time, more than one hundred and forty students in residence.... it is only desired to show here how the prediction of building the largest Bible College in the country by prayer and faith alone *was fulfilled.*' (My emphasis).

In addition, two local newspapers the *Evening Post* and the *Western Mail* published an article in January 1932 which stated: 'The College is one of the strongest and most impressive examples of faith manifested by works in modern religious history.' (Chapter 9 of *God Challenges the Dictators*).

Rees Howells commissioned the architect D. Glyn Williams of Swansea in early 1934 to draw up designs for two student blocks, one to accommodate 700 men and the other for 300 women. Rees Howells had his sights set on accommodation for 1,000 students and was inspired by the 900-student, Moody Bible Institute in Chicago, America, when Rees and Lizzie Howells visited in and around spring 1923. This was their second trip to America together, having done deputation work for the South African General Mission in the early 1920s.

2. The *South African Pioneer* (Nov. 1916) notes Rees and Lizzie Howells' employment was from 1914. After nearly two years of preparation and training at separate establishments, they left Britain for the mission field in July 1915.

Chapter 9

1. The Bible College of Wales (BCW) was incorrectly known by a number of names including Blackpill Bible College, Swansea Bible College and Wales Bible College all of which denote the location of the College. Early postcards called the Glynderwen site: Blackpill Bible College or Blackpyll Bible College. The Glynderwen Estate was on the boundary of Blackpill and Sketty (though technically within Blackpill) depending on which entrance you used to access

the grounds. Derwen Fawr and Sketty Isaf, were a five minute walk away and were firmly located in (lower) Sketty, however, some early postcards have a photo of the Derwen Fawr Mansion, with 'Bible College – Derwen Fawr Blackpill' in white text written on the front of the postcards. Mail sent from the United Kingdom and abroad to BCW was sometimes sent to other Bible Colleges in Wales; some were redirected to BCW whilst others were returned to the sender. Samuel Rees Howells sent 100s of letters annually to former students, staff and workers at other Christian organisations. On occasions, those on the mission field (or in the UK) who wrote to thank Samuel Rees Howells had their mail sent to another Bible College in Wales, some mail was forwarded to BCW at Swansea. Some overseas people would have "South Wales" on the bottom of their airmail envelope instead of United Kingdom or Great Britain and one Christian worker had his mail sent to New South Wales (having written South Wales at the bottom) and redirected back to his home in America!

2. Rees and Lizzie Howells saw Niagara Falls when they visited America on a private trip in and around spring 1923. They had a studio photo taken of themselves at the "Falls," this was the driest and clearest option!

Chapter 10

1. The phrase and statement: 'The Waves and the Winds beat upon the Rock of Faith but the Rock stands firm, serenely confident. For is it not the Rock of Ages?' is an allusion to the Parable of the Wise and Foolish Builder (Matthew 7:24-27 and Luke 6:46-49). God is known as a Rock (Deuteronomy 32:4, 18, 31, 1 Samuel 2:2, 2 Samuel 22:2, 32, 2 Samuel 23:3, Psalm 18:46 and Psalm 28:1). Jesus Christ is also known as a Rock (Romans 9:33, 1 Corinthians 10:4 and 1 Peter 2:8). In addition, *Rock of Ages* is also the title of a hymn by August Toplady, written in 1763, as he sheltered in the cleft of a rock at Burrington Combe during a storm. The hymn was based on Psalm 94:22 and was first published in 1775. This cleft in a rock in the Mendipp Hills is now known as Rock of Ages and has a plaque in place retelling this famous incident. The Psalmist declared, "But the Lord is my defence; and my God is the Rock of my refuge" (Psalm 94:22). Jesus said: "And why call ye Me, Lord, Lord, and do not the things which I say? Whosoever cometh to me, and heareth my sayings, and doeth them, I will shew you to whom he is like. He is like a man which built a house, and digged deep, and laid the foundation on a rock: and when the flood arose, the stream beat vehemently upon that house, and could not shake it: for it was founded upon a rock. But he that heareth, and doeth not, is like a man that without a foundation built a house upon the earth; against which the stream did beat vehemently, and immediately it fell; and the ruin of that house was great" (Luke 6:46-49).

2. The Bible College in Paris was called Maison de l'Evangile (The Gospel House) in Bois-de-Boulogne, Paris, France. Originally it was known by the Bible College of Wales as the Wakefield Bible College after a previous owner Thomas Wakefield Richardson. It cost Rees Howells the equivalent of £10,000 to buy in 1938 (£674,400 in 2020, though the value of the property is considerably more) and officially became BCW property in January 1939. See *Samuel, Son and Successor of Rees Howells: Director of the Bible College of Wales – A Biography* by Richard Maton, ByFaith Media, 2012, 2018, chapter 24. Within the book by Richard Maton are additional references to other Colleges and organisations which were associated to or had ties to the Bible College of Wales (BCW) in Beirut, Lebanon and Ramallah in the Holy Land.

In addition, some former BCW students and staff were sent regular financial gifts (three to six times a year appears standard) by Rees Howells and then under his son, Samuel Rees Howells. Some of these former students founded training organisations or ministries which were often seen as extensions of BCW, being founded and run along the same principles of the 'life of faith' and the 'Every Creature Commission.' Jesus said, Go and make disciples of all nations' (Matthew 28:19). Finances from BCW were sent to other Bible Colleges and Training Centres in the United Kingdom and abroad. Rees Howells in *God Challenges the Dictators* wrote: 'The Lord is going to prepare hundreds of young people, who, after spending three or four years in the Bible College of Wales, will go out and found Colleges in every country to reach Every Creature; men and women.... Then, instead of only a few missionaries and native workers, working on lonely stations, there will be thousands (including natives), trained in the Colleges, available for missionary work.' (Chapter 8).

Chapter 11
1. See footnote 4. under chapter 12 in Sources and Notes.
2. The phrase 'for Him who commanded His thoughtless disciples to let the little ones come unto Him' is an allusion to an incident recorded in the Holy Bible with Jesus, His disciples and multiple parents bringing their young children for Him to bless them. 'Then little children were brought to Him that He might put His hands on them and pray, but the disciples rebuked them. But Jesus said, "Let the little children come to Me, and do not forbid them; for of such is the Kingdom of Heaven." And He laid His hands on them and departed from there' (Matthew 19:13-15).

Chapter 12
1. Jerry McAuley (1839-1884), along with his wife Maria, founded the Walter Street Mission in New York City in October 1872. It was America's first Rescue Mission, originally known as Helping Hand for Men based at 316 Walter Street, and is now known as the New York City Rescue Mission. Jerry McAuley was a self-described "rogue and street thief" who in the late 1850s was sentenced to spend fourteen years in Sing Sing Prison in Ossining, New York. He was the son of a counterfeiter from Ireland who fled home, and Jerry aged thirteen was sent to America to live with his older sister. He 'worked' with gangs to survive and was eventually caught and sentenced in 1857. He was converted in prison by reading his Bible and through the visits of a lady missionary who shared the Good News with him. The power of Jesus Christ transformed his life so much that he was released after serving seven years and two months, less than half his time. His Rescue Mission at 316 Walter Street held nightly meetings in the slum area of New York and anybody and everybody was allowed to enter, however drunk, dirty or smelly. The power of Christ to save and transform was preached, testimonies were given and there was singing to rouse the souls of those present.
2. These are two stanzas from the hymn *Under His Wings* by James L. Nicholson and can be found in *Sacred Songs and Solos* by I. D. Sankey, 1878. The hymn is also known as *In God I have Found a Retreat* from its first line.
3. The phrase "Where He leads Me I Will Follow" is a missionary adage and is used in two hymns (Lou W. Wilson's *I'll Follow Where He Leads* and George W. Collins' *I Have Heard My Savior calling*, and is the refrain in a third hymn, E. W. Blandy's *Where He Leads Me*. Many short-term missioners (STM-ers) add as a second line: "What He feeds Me I Will Swallow." For STMs see *Short-Term*

Missions, A Christian Guide to STMs by Mathew Backholer, ByFaith Media, 2016.

4. The Founders only child whom they left behind in Wales when they went to Africa was Samuel. If they had taken him to Africa he would have probably died of malaria or some fever. Africa was known as the "White Man's Graveyard" for a very good reason. The author first met Samuel, this man of God, when Samuel was in his 80s and his story is told in: *Samuel, Son and Successor of Rees Howells: Director of the Bible College of Wales – A Biography* by Richard Maton, ByFaith Media, 2012, 2018, and *Samuel Rees Howells A Life of Intercession: The Legacy of Prayer and Spiritual Warfare of an Intercessor* by Richard Maton, Paul Backholer and Mathew Backholer, ByFaith Media, 2012, 2018.

5. See footnote 1. under chapter 6 in Sources and Notes.

6. The Home of Rest for Missionaries was in Sketty Isaf whilst the Hospital in which to nurse missionaries was on the Derwen Fawr Estate. These two sites were opposite each other and divided by the Derwen Fawr Road. The Home of Rest for Missionaries was often full and priority for the Hospital was for missionaries. By November 1937 there were around 250 school children at the School and 120 resident students at the Bible College, so very full. Below are excerpts of two letters from April and November 1937 and one from May 1943.

Evan and Florence Howells (no relation), missionaries to Angola, Africa, wrote to Rees Howells as they were on furlough, desiring to visit, and received a reply by return of post on 14th April 1937: 'Dear Mr and Mrs Howells, delighted to hear that you are back in the country.... We shall be very pleased to see you when you come this way. There is always a "Prophet's Chamber" for the Missionaries, so please send me a card when you will be coming. With Christian greetings, yours sincerely, [Rees Howells].'

In a letter to Dublin, dated 30th November 1937, Rees Howells wrote: 'Your letter to hand regarding your sister. We regret that the Missionary Home and College are both very full, just now and it will be impossible for anyone to give personal attention to your sister. Nearly every bed is taken up, and although we have to give *a great deal of attention to the missionaries who come back on furlough and are sick*, [my emphasis] but the nurses are giving their attention to them, so that when your sister comes it would be advisable for someone to come with her. So under the circumstances it would perhaps be better for your sister to come later on, as the winter is really the worst time. Your Sincerely, [Rees Howells].'

In a letter, dated 22nd May 1943, Rees Howells wrote to Corporal C. Workman of Shrewsbury, England, and mentions an 86-year-old missionary to Japan, Miss Evans, who 'is enjoying the provision that the Lord has made for her' in the Missionary Home.

7. Many children were born in the College Hospital. This was pre-NHS when healthcare had to be paid for across Britain. As a thank you to Britain for the sacrifices that had been made during World War II, the National Health Service (which became known as the NHS) sprang into being on 5th July 1948, and seeing a doctor or receiving medical attention in a NHS Hospital was free.

8. This couple came to BCW in and around the mid-1930s under Rees Howells' leadership. In mid-1964, they were missionaries in South Rhodesia and under the leadership of Samuel Rees Howells he was sending them financial support.

9. Rees Howells intended to build a 'large Hospital, for two hundred patients...on the new estate, Penllergaer,' but this never happened. American officers (and soldiers) were based at Penllergaer from 1943 and officers lived in the Big House, the Mansion and it was badly damaged during their occupation.

As examples: Chunks of marble were smashed from the twin marble staircase, presumably by dragging heavy objects like metal filing cabinets down or up them! Whilst the brick astronomical observatory built in 1846, from where some of the earliest photos of the moon (1857) were taken was used as target practice! Evidence of the bullet marks can still be seen in this preserved and recently renovated, historical building.

Chapter 13
1. See footnote 2. under chapter 10 in Sources and Notes.
2. The phrase 'Peace at Eventide' means a 'Literary Evening,' an old fashioned phrase for the last section in a book.
3. On 7th November 1945, Rees Howells wrote to Rev. S. H. Dixon in Edinburgh House, London. In part of the letter he wrote: 'I also said in the book [*God Challenges the Dictators*] that as a thank-offering for victory over the dictators and those systems, that I was to give £100,000 to build Colleges and Schools in the Holy Land. All I need today to get this £100,000 is to sell one of the estates and it will be in my hands to give. Although since the book was written I have been led of the Lord to give Penllergaer Mansion and 54 acres of land to the war orphans. The Mansion itself is valued at £20,000 [£864,900 in 2020] and I am giving it as a gift to Barnardo's.'

Barnardo's looked at the Penllergaer Mansion and 54 acres and stated that it would be too expensive for them to convert it into a children's home. In addition, large children's homes were becoming a thing of the past, giving way to smaller groups of children in family friendly styled settings. In a sermon from spring 1944 Rees Howells spoke about a building that Barnardo's had bought in Lyndhurst to house 40 children, but the Council would not permit them to use it as a home. However, in the previous year, the Annesley Bank Barnardo's Home in Pinkney Lane, Lyndhurst, Hampshire was opened, Barnardo's having obtained it in 1939. http://www.childrenshomes.org.uk/LyndhurstDB/. Accessed 12 October 2019. There was a Barnardo's Home in Shaftsbury House, Swansea for 'little boys' which was opened in 1902. *Memoirs of the Late Dr Barnardo* by Syrie Louise Elmsie Barnardo, 1907.
4. 'The sands of time are sinking, The dawn of Heaven breaks' was originally a poem of 19 stanzas by Ann Ross Cousin and was first published in *The Christian Treasury* (1857). Rees Howells quoted a single stanza of what became a hymn entitled *The Sands of Time Are Sinking* popular with just six stanzas.

Epilogue
1. *Rees Howells Intercessor* by Norman Grubb, Lutterworth Press, 1952, page 241.

Blow the trumpet in Zion, and sound an alarm in My holy mountain! Let all the inhabitants of the land tremble; for the day of the Lord is coming, for it is at hand' (Joel 2:1).

---

www.ByFaith.org

www.ByFaithBooks.org

www.ByFaithDVDs.org

ByFaith Media Books

The following ByFaith Media books are available as paperbacks and eBooks, whilst some are available as hardbacks.

Biography and Autobiography

9781907066-14-6. *Samuel, Son and Successor of Rees Howells: Director of the Bible College of Wales – A Biography* by Richard Maton. The life of Samuel and his ministry at the College and the support he received from numerous staff and students as the history of BCW unfolds. With 113 black and white photos. Hardback 9781907066-36-8.

9781907066-41-2. *The Holy Spirit in a Man: Spiritual Warfare, Intercession, Faith, Healings and Miracles* by R. B. Watchman. One man's compelling journey of faith and intercession, a remarkable modern day story of miracles and faith to inspire and encourage. (One chapter relates to the Bible College of Wales and Watchman's visit).

9781907066-13-9. *Samuel Rees Howells A Life of Intercession: The Legacy of Prayer and Spiritual Warfare of an Intercessor* by Richard Maton, Paul Backholer and Mathew Backholer is an in-depth look at the intercessions of Samuel Rees Howells alongside the faith principles that he learnt from his father, Rees Howells, and under the leading and guidance of the Holy Spirit. With 39 black and white photographs. Hardback 9781907066-37-5.

Christian Teaching and Inspirational

9781907066-35-1. *Jesus Today, Daily Devotional: 100 Days with Jesus Christ* by Paul Backholer. One hundred days of two minutes of Christian inspiration to draw you closer to God to encourage and inspire. Have you ever wished you could have sat at Jesus' feet and heard Him speak? *Jesus Today* is a concise daily devotional defined by Jesus' teaching and how His life can change ours. See the world from God's perspective, learn who Jesus was, what He preached and what it means to live abundantly in Christ.

9781907066-33-7. *Holy Spirit Power: Knowing the Voice, Guidance and Person of the Holy Spirit* by Paul Backholer. Power for Christian living; drawing from the powerful influences of many Christian leaders, including: Rees Howells, Evan Roberts, D. L. Moody, Duncan Campbell and other channels of God's Divine fire.

9781907066-43-6. *Tares and Weeds in Your Church: Trouble & Deception in God's House, the End Time Overcomers* by R. B. Watchman. Is there a battle taking place in your house, church or ministry, leading to division? Tares and weeds are counterfeit Christians used to sabotage Kingdom work; learn how to recognise them and neutralise them in the power of the Holy Spirit.

9781907066-56-6. *The Baptism of Fire, Personal Revival, Renewal and the Anointing for Supernatural Living* by Paul Backholer. Jesus will baptise you with the Holy Spirit and fire; that was the promise of John the Baptist. But what is the baptism of fire and how can you experience it? The author unveils the life and ministry of the Holy Spirit, shows how He can transform your life and what supernatural living in Christ means.

Historical
9781907066-78-8. *Rees Howells' God Challenges the Dictators, Doom of Axis Powers Predicted: Victory for Christian England and Release of Europe Through Intercession and Spiritual Warfare, Bible College of Wales* by Mathew Backholer. This is the story behind the story of *God Challenges the Dictators* (GCD), Rees Howells' only published book, before, during and after publication which is centred around World War II. Read how extracts of GCD were aired over occupied parts of Europe, and how Hitler and leading Nazi officials were sent copies in 1940! The book includes letters to Winston Churchill and Press Releases from Rees Howells and how he sent copies of his book to Prime Ministers N. Chamberlain and W. Churchill plus government officials, and what the newspapers had to say, at home and abroad, as afar away as Australia and the Oceanic Islands! With twenty-four black and white photos.

9781907066-76-4. Hardback collector's edition. *God Challenges the Dictators, Doom of the Nazis Predicted: The Destruction of the Third Reich Foretold by the Director of Swansea Bible College, An Intercessor from Wales* by Rees Howells and Mathew Backholer. Available for the first time in 80 years – fully annotated and reformatted with twelve digitally enhanced black and white photos. Discover how Rees Howells built a large ministry by faith in times of economic chaos and learn from the predictions he made during times of national crisis, of the destruction of the Third Reich, the end of fascism and the liberation of Christian Europe during World War II. Also available as a paperback 978-1-907066-77-1.

978-1-907066-95-5. Hardback collector's edition. *Rees Howells, Vision Hymns of Spiritual Warfare & Intercessory Declarations: World War II Songs of Victory, Intercession, Praise and Worship, Israel and the Every Creature Commission* by Mathew Backholer. A collection of rare hymns and choruses from the Bible College of Wales (BCW) under Rees Howells' Directorship composed by different people. Drawn from three different BCW hymn books spanning the pivotal years of 1939-1948 and brought to life for the first time in more than seventy years.

Many of the hymns reveal the theology, spiritual battles, and history during the dark days of World War II and the years surrounding it.

9781907066-45-0. *Britain, A Christian Country, A Nation Defined by Christianity and the Bible & the Social Changes that Challenge this Biblical Heritage* by Paul Backholer. For more than 1,000 years Britain was defined by Christianity, with monarch's dedicating the country to God and national days of prayer. Discover this continuing legacy, how faith defined its nationhood and the challenges from the 1960s till today.

9781907066-02-3. *How Christianity Made the Modern World* by Paul Backholer. Christianity is the greatest reforming force that the world has ever known, yet its legacy is seldom comprehended. But now, using personal observations and worldwide research the author brings this legacy alive by revealing how Christianity helped create the path that led to Western liberty and laid the foundations of the modern world.

9781907066-47-4. *Celtic Christianity & the First Christian Kings in Britain: From St. Patrick and St. Columba, to King Ethelbert and King Alfred* by Paul Backholer. Celtic Christians ignited a Celtic Golden Age of faith and light which spread into Europe. Discover this striking history and what we can learn from the heroes of Celtic Christianity.

Biblical Adventure and Archaeology
9781907066-52-8. *Lost Treasures of the Bible: Exploration and Pictorial Travel Adventure of Biblical Archaeology* by Paul Backholer. Unveil ancient mysteries as you discover the evidence for Israel's exodus from Egypt, and travel into lost civilizations in search of the Ark of the Covenant. Explore lost worlds with over 160 colour photos and pictures.

978178822-000-2. *The Exodus Evidence In Pictures – The Bible's Exodus: The Hunt for Ancient Israel in Egypt, the Red Sea, the Exodus Route and Mount Sinai* by Paul Backholer. Two brothers and explorers, Paul and Mathew Backholer search for archaeological data to validate the biblical account of Joseph, Moses and the Hebrew Exodus from ancient Egypt. With more than 100 full colour photos and graphics!

978178822-001-9. *The Ark of the Covenant – Investigating the Ten Leading Claims* by Paul Backholer. Join two explorers as they investigate the ten major theories concerning the location of antiquities greatest relic. Combining an on-site travel journal with 80+ colour photographs through Egypt, Ethiopia and beyond.

Revivals and Spiritual Awakenings
9781907066-01-6. *Revival Fires and Awakenings, Thirty-Six Visitations of the Holy Spirit: A Call to Holiness, Prayer and Intercession for the Nations* by Mathew Backholer. With thirty-six fascinating accounts of

revivals in nineteen countries from six continents, plus biblical teaching on revival, prayer and intercession. Also available as a hardback 9781907066-38-2.

9781907066-07-8. *Global Revival, Worldwide Outpourings, Forty-Three Visitations of the Holy Spirit: The Great Commission* by Mathew Backholer. How revivals are birthed and the fascinating links between pioneering missionaries and the revivals that they saw as they worked towards the Great Commission, with forty-three accounts of revivals.

9781907066-00-9. *Understanding Revival and Addressing the Issues it Provokes* by Mathew Backholer. Everything you need to know about revival and its phenomena. How to work with the Holy Spirit to see God rend the Heavens and pour out His Spirit on a dry and thirsty land and how not to be taken in by the enemy and his counterfeit tricks, delusions and imitations.

9781907066-06-1. *Revival Fire, 150 Years of Revivals, Spiritual Awakenings and Moves of the Holy Spirit* by Mathew Backholer. This book documents in detail, twelve revivals from ten countries on five continents. Be inspired, encouraged and challenged.

9781907066-15-3. *Revival Answers, True and False Revivals, Genuine or Counterfeit Do not be Deceived* by Mathew Backholer. What is genuine revival and how can we tell the true from the spurious? Drawing from Scripture with examples across Church history, this book will sharpen your senses and take you on a journey of discovery.

9781907066-60-3. *Reformation to Revival, 500 Years of God's Glory: Sixty Revivals Awakenings and Heaven-Sent visitations of the Holy Spirit* by Mathew Backholer. *Reformation to Revival* traces the Divine thread of God's power from Martin Luther of 1517, through to the Charismatic Movement and into the twenty-first century, with sixty great revivals.

Christian Discipleship
9781907066-62-7. *Christianity Rediscovered, in Pursuit of God and the Path to Eternal Life: What you Need to Know to Grow, Living the Christian Life with Jesus Christ, Book 1* by Mathew Backholer. Since the beginning of time mankind has asked, "Why am I alive, does my life matter and is there an afterlife I can prepare for?" *Christianity Rediscovered* has the answers and will help you find meaning, focus, clarity and peace.

9781907066-12-2. *Discipleship For Everyday Living, Christian Growth: Following Jesus Christ and Making Disciples of All Nations* by Mathew Backholer. Engaging biblical teaching to aid Christian believers in maturity, to help make strong disciples with solid biblical foundations who reflect the image of Jesus Christ.

9781907066-16-0. *Extreme Faith, On Fire Christianity: Hearing from God and Moving in His Grace, Strength & Power – Living in Victory* by Mathew Backholer. Discover the powerful biblical foundations for on-fire faith in Christ! This book explores biblical truths and routines to shake your world.

Short-Term Missions (Christian Travel with a Purpose)

9781907066-49-8. *Short-Term Missions, A Christian Guide to STMs: For Leaders, Pastors, Churches, Students, STM Teams and Mission Organizations – Survive and Thrive!* by Mathew Backholer. A concise guide to Short-Term Missions (STMs). What you need to know about planning a STM, or joining a STM team, and considering the options as part of the Great Commission, from the Good News to good works.

9781907066-05-4. *How to Plan, Prepare and Successfully Complete Your Short-Term Mission For Churches, Independent STM Teams and Mission Organizations* by Mathew Backholer. This book will guide you through all you need to know about STMs and includes: mission statistics, cultural issues, where and when to go, what to do and pack, food, accommodation, and more than 140 real-life STM testimonies.

Supernatural and Spiritual

9781907066-58-0. *Glimpses of Glory, Revelations in the Realms of God Beyond the Veil in the Heavenly Abode: The New Jerusalem and the Eternal Kingdom of God* by Paul Backholer. Find a world beyond earth which is real, vivid and eternal. A gripping read!

9781907066-18-4. *Prophecy Now, Prophetic Words and Divine Revelations for You, the Church and the Nations* by Michael Backholer. An enlightening end-time prophetic journal of visions, prophecies and words from the Holy Spirit to God's people, the Church and the nations.

9781907066-80-1. *Heaven, Paradise is Real, Hope Beyond Death: An Angelic Pilgrimage to Your Future Home* by Paul Backholer. Come on a journey to another world of eternal bliss, joy and light, in this enchanting narrative which pulls you in and shows you heaven. Meet those who have gone before into paradise and found eternal peace. Enter into the heavenly Jerusalem, with a man and an angelic guide to discover the truth about immortality, the afterlife and the joy of eternity.

Budget Travel – Vacation/Holiday

9781907066-54-2. *Budget Travel, a Guide to Travelling on a Shoestring, Explore the World, a Discount Overseas Adventure Trip: Gap Year, Backpacking, Volunteer-Vacation and Overlander* by Mathew Backholer. *Budget Travel* is a practical and concise guide to travelling the world and exploring new destinations with fascinating opportunities and experiences. Full of anecdotes, traveller's advice, informative timelines and testimonies, with suggestions, guidance and ideas.

9781907066-74-0. *Travel the World and Explore for Less than $50 a Day, the Essential Guide: Your Budget Backpack Global Adventure, from Two Weeks to a Gap Year, Solo or with Friends* by Mathew Backholer. A practical guide for the solo backpacker or with friends that will save you time and money with ideas, and need-to-know information so you can have the adventure of a lifetime from two weeks to one year.

ByFaith Media DVDs

Revivals and Spiritual Awakenings
9781907066-03-0. *Great Christian Revivals* on 1 DVD is an inspirational and uplifting account of some of the greatest revivals in Church history. Filmed on location across Britain and drawing upon archive information, the stories of the Welsh Revival (1904-1905), the Hebridean Revival (1949-1952) and the Evangelical Revival (1739-1791) are brought to life in this moving 72-minute documentary. Using computer animation, historic photos and depictions, the events of the past are weaved into the present, to bring these Heaven-sent revivals to life.

Christian Travel (Backpacking Short-Term Missions)
9781907066-04-7. *ByFaith – World Mission* on 1 DVD is a Christian reality TV show that reveals the real experience of backpacking short-term missions in Asia, Europe and North Africa. Two brothers, Paul and Mathew Backholer shoot through fourteen nations, in an 85-minute real-life documentary. Filmed over three years, *ByFaith – World Mission* is the best of ByFaith TV season one.

Historical and Adventure
9781907066-09-2. *Israel in Egypt – The Exodus Mystery* on 1 DVD. A four year quest searching for Joseph, Moses and the Hebrew slaves in Egypt. Join brothers Paul and Mathew Backholer as they hunt through ancient relics and explore the mystery of the biblical exodus, hunt for the Red Sea and climb Mount Sinai. Discover the first reference to Israel outside of the Bible, uncover depictions of people with multicoloured coats, encounter the Egyptian records of slaves making bricks and find lost cities. 110 minutes. The best of *ByFaith – In Search of the Exodus*.

9781907066-10-0. *ByFaith – Quest for the Ark of the Covenant* on 1 DVD. Join two adventurers on their quest for the Ark, beginning at Mount Sinai where it was made, to Pharaoh Tutankhamun's tomb, where Egyptian treasures evoke the majesty of the Ark. The quest proceeds onto the trail of Pharaoh Shishak, who raided Jerusalem. The mission continues up the River Nile to find a lost temple, with clues to a mysterious civilization. Crossing through the Sahara Desert, the investigators enter the underground rock churches of Ethiopia, find a forgotten civilization and examine the enigma of the final resting place of the Ark itself. 100+ minutes.

www.ByFaithDVDs.org

ByFaith Media Downloads and Streaming

The following ByFaith Media productions are based on the DVDs from the previous page and are available to download: to buy, rent or to stream via Amazon.

Revivals and Spiritual Awakenings
Glorious Christian Revival and Holy Spirit Awakenings: The Welsh, Hebridean and Evangelical Revivals, Evan Roberts, Duncan Campbell and John Wesley. 1 hour 12 minutes. Discover the Welsh Revival (1904-1905), the Hebridean Revival (1949-1952) and the Evangelical Revival (1739-1791), with Evan Roberts, Duncan Campbell, John and Charles Wesley, George Whitefield and others. Filmed on location across the UK and beyond. B07N2N762J (UK). B07P1TVY6W (USA).

Christian Travel (Backpacking Short-Term Missions)
Short-Term Mission Adventures, A Global Christian Missionary STM Expedition with brothers Mathew and Paul Backholer. 1 hour 15 minutes. The mission begins when two adventurers land in Asia, a continent of maximum extremes. After overcoming culture shock and difficult travel, the adventurous missionaries preach in the slums. From India they strike out into Nepal, Bangladesh, Thailand, Myanmar, Cambodia and Vietnam. The mission also touches down in the great cities of Europe: London, Paris, Rome, Dublin, Frankfurt & Amsterdam. B07N2PVZZK (UK). B07PNSWBKN (USA).

Historical and Adventure
The Bible's Lost Ark of the Covenant: Where Is It? Egypt, Ethiopia or Israel? With brothers Mathew and Paul Backholer. 1 hour 10 minutes. The Ark of the Covenant was the greatest treasure in Solomon's Temple, but when Jerusalem fell the Ark vanished from history. Now join two adventurers on their quest for the Ark of the Covenant, beginning at Mount Sinai where it was made, to Pharaoh Tutankhamun's tomb, crossing the Sahara Desert into the underground rock churches of Ethiopia and beyond in an epic adventure. B07MTTHHZ7 (UK). B07R3BMBW6 (USA).

The Exodus Evidence: Quest for Ancient Israel in Egypt, The Red Sea, The Exodus Route & Mount Sinai. Join two adventurers, brothers Mathew and Paul Backholer as they investigate a three-thousand year old mystery, entering the tombs of ancient Egypt seeking the exodus evidence. Discover the first reference to Israel outside of the Bible in hieroglyphics, uncover ancient depictions of people with multi-colored coats, encounter the Egyptian records of slaves making bricks and find lost cities mentioned in the Bible. 1 hour 15 minutes. B07P63BWZ2 (UK). B07Q3ST613 (USA).

Online Exclusive (not to rent or buy)

Christian Revival & Holy Spirit Awakenings. Join revival historian and prolific author Mathew Backholer, as he joins CEO Gordon Pettie in the Revelation TV studios over 7 episodes to examine many powerful Christian revivals which shook the world. Including the: Layman's Prayer Revival of 1857, Ulster Revival 1859-60, Welsh Revival of 1904-05, Azusa Street Revival of 1906-09, Korean Revival of 1907-10, the Hebridean Revival of 1949-52 and more! B07R766FQL (UK). Coming to the USA soon!

Notes

CPSIA information can be obtained
at www.ICGtesting.com
Printed in the USA
LVHW020958031122
732161LV00012B/685